国立高専
過去10年分　入試問題集

英　語

（問題は各年度、50分で行って下さ

JN014058

目　次

（キリトリ線に沿って、切り取ってお使い下さい。）

1　次の各組の英文がほぼ同じ意味を表すように，（ A ）と（ B ）に入れるのに最も適当な組み合わせをア〜エの中から一つずつ選びなさい。

（1）Plants and animals （ A ） water to live.

Plants and animals cannot live （ B ） water.

ア $\begin{cases} \text{(A) want} \\ \text{(B) on} \end{cases}$ イ $\begin{cases} \text{(A) drink} \\ \text{(B) by} \end{cases}$ ウ $\begin{cases} \text{(A) need} \\ \text{(B) without} \end{cases}$ エ $\begin{cases} \text{(A) use} \\ \text{(B) for} \end{cases}$

（2）This castle was （ A ） four hundred years ago.

This castle is four hundred years （ B ） now.

ア $\begin{cases} \text{(A) building} \\ \text{(B) age} \end{cases}$ イ $\begin{cases} \text{(A) making} \\ \text{(B) building} \end{cases}$ ウ $\begin{cases} \text{(A) made} \\ \text{(B) from} \end{cases}$ エ $\begin{cases} \text{(A) built} \\ \text{(B) old} \end{cases}$

（3）Tom is （ A ） strong that he can carry the heavy box.

Tom is strong （ B ） to carry the heavy box.

ア $\begin{cases} \text{(A) too} \\ \text{(B) more} \end{cases}$ イ $\begin{cases} \text{(A) so} \\ \text{(B) enough} \end{cases}$ ウ $\begin{cases} \text{(A) very} \\ \text{(B) most} \end{cases}$ エ $\begin{cases} \text{(A) such} \\ \text{(B) much} \end{cases}$

（4）I'm a （ A ） cook.

I can't cook （ B ）.

ア $\begin{cases} \text{(A) nice} \\ \text{(B) good} \end{cases}$ イ $\begin{cases} \text{(A) wrong} \\ \text{(B) bad} \end{cases}$ ウ $\begin{cases} \text{(A) poor} \\ \text{(B) well} \end{cases}$ エ $\begin{cases} \text{(A) better} \\ \text{(B) much} \end{cases}$

（5）（ A ） you don't hurry up, you will miss the last bus.

Hurry up, （ B ） you will miss the last bus.

ア $\begin{cases} \text{(A) If} \\ \text{(B) or} \end{cases}$ イ $\begin{cases} \text{(A) Though} \\ \text{(B) but} \end{cases}$ ウ $\begin{cases} \text{(A) When} \\ \text{(B) however} \end{cases}$ エ $\begin{cases} \text{(A) Because} \\ \text{(B) and} \end{cases}$

2 次の1〜5の会話文の（　　　　　）に入る適切なものを，ア〜エの中から一つずつ選びなさい。

1　A : Excuse me. Can you tell me where the city library is?

　　B : I'm sorry. I'm just visiting here.

　　A : Oh, I see. (　　　　　)

　　ア　I'll visit here.　　　　　　　　イ　Here you are.

　　ウ　I'll ask someone else.　　　　　エ　Help yourself.

2　A : Hello. This is John. May I speak to Mr. Tanaka?

　　B : Sorry, but he's not here now. (　　　　　)

　　A : Yes, please. Could you tell him that I'll be late for school?

　　ア　Can I leave a message?　　　　　イ　Can I take a message?

　　ウ　Can I tell you something?　　　　エ　Can I ask you something?

3　A : Here is a T-shirt I bought for you in Tokyo.

　　B : Thank you. Where in Tokyo did you buy it?

　　A : In Harajuku. (　　　　　)

　　B : Just once. I enjoyed shopping along the street.

　　ア　Have you ever been there?　　　イ　When did you buy it?

　　ウ　How did you go there?　　　　　エ　Where have you been?

4　A : We are planning to go swimming this Sunday. Would you like to come?

　　B : Thanks, but I'm busy this weekend.

　　A : That's too bad. (　　　　　)

　　B : OK. Can I bring my brother with me?

　　A : Sure.

　　ア　How about next Saturday?　　　イ　Last Sunday was nice.

　　ウ　Are you tired?　　　　　　　　エ　Have a good time.

5　A : We will have a birthday party for Lisa in the afternoon. Will you help me?

　　B : OK, Mom. How can I help you?

　　A : Will you put the cups on the table?

　　B : Sure. (　　　　　)

　　A : Six, please.

　　ア　How old are they?　　　　　　イ　How much do you need?

　　ウ　How often do you need?　　　　エ　How many do you need?

3　次の文章は，ロケット（rocket）の製作に情熱を傾けたアメリカ人 Robert Goddard に関する ものです。これをよく読んで，後の問いに答えなさい。

Robert Goddard was one of the first American scientists who believed that rockets could fly to the moon. Before Goddard was born, rockets were only used as fireworks or as weapons in wars. Most scientists didn't think that rockets could （ 1 ） to travel into space.

Robert Goddard first started thinking about using rockets for space travel in high school. He graduated from high school in 1904 and made his first rocket while he was a university student. It didn't fly, but he （ 2 ） trying.

Goddard studied hard and became a teacher at a university. One day, he wrote a report about his ideas. In the report, he said that rockets could go to the moon someday. But in 1920, he read a story in *The New York Times* newspaper and was （ 3 ）. The story said that Goddard was wrong and rockets could never fly into space. It also said that even high school students knew （ 4 ） about science than Goddard.

Goddard was angry and worked harder to make better rockets. He wanted to make a new kind of rocket （ 5 ） used a special fuel. Finally, （ 6 ） March 16, 1926, his new rocket flew 12 meters high.

Goddard never made a rocket that could fly to the moon, but he had many good ideas. He died in 1945. Later, scientists used his ideas to make bigger and better rockets. When the first men walked on the moon in 1969, *The New York Times* newspaper finally said Goddard's ideas were right.

（注）firework 花火　　　　weapon 武器　　　　space 宇宙　　　　graduate 卒業する
　　　The New York Times　ニューヨークタイムズ社（米国の新聞社）　　fuel 燃料

問1　本文中の（ 1 ）～（ 6 ）に入れるのに適切なものを，ア～エの中から一つずつ選びなさい。

（ 1 ）	ア	use	イ	used	ウ	be used	エ	be using
（ 2 ）	ア	hoped	イ	kept	ウ	stopped	エ	wanted
（ 3 ）	ア	agreed	イ	learned	ウ	shocked	エ	watched
（ 4 ）	ア	little	イ	many	ウ	much	エ	more
（ 5 ）	ア	that	イ	these	ウ	this	エ	those
（ 6 ）	ア	at	イ	in	ウ	on	エ	with

問2　本文の内容と合うものを次のア～オの中から二つ選びなさい。

ア　When Goddard was a high school student, he studied fireworks as weapons.

イ　Goddard made his first rocket when he was a university student.

ウ　Goddard became a high school teacher after he graduated from university.

エ　Goddard was the first man who made a rocket which could fly to the moon.

オ　An American newspaper said Goddard's ideas were right after he died.

4　次の１〜５の会話文の（　　）内の語句を並べ替え，それぞれの文を完成しなさい。解答は，（　　）内において３番目と５番目にくるものの記号を選びなさい。なお，文頭にくる語も小文字で書かれています。

1　A：This temple is famous for its beautiful garden.
　　B：I know. I（ア are　イ heard　ウ on　エ painted　オ the pictures　カ the walls）also
　　　beautiful.

2　A：（ア for　イ minutes　ウ more　エ than　オ twenty　カ walking）every day is good for
　　　our health.
　　B：Yes. I run every morning.

3　A：It's so cold today. Will you（ア drink　イ give　ウ hot　エ me　オ something　カ to）?
　　B：OK. How about hot milk?

4　A：Excuse me.（ア arrive　イ at　ウ train　エ Yokohama　オ which　カ will）before
　　　noon?
　　B：Take the next train on Track 2.

5　A：（ア does　イ from　ウ how　エ it　オ long　カ take）here to the city museum by taxi?
　　B：About ten minutes.

5　次の文章および下の表をよく読んで，後の問いに答えなさい。なお，解答に際しては，問題文に書かれている事実以外を考慮する必要はありません。

Takashi is a junior high school student. He lives with his parents and a sister. His sister is a college student. Mayumi is Takashi's classmate. She lives next to his house. Mayumi has a sister, too. She is an elementary school student. The two families like movies very much.

One Friday afternoon, Takashi's family went to a movie theater. They arrived there at four thirty and chose movies to see. Takashi and his father hurried to buy their tickets because their movie was going to begin in a few minutes. The movie started as soon as they sat in their seats. Takashi's sister chose a different movie and her mother also liked it. They bought tickets and waited for about half an hour before their movie started. After the family enjoyed the movies, they went home together.

The next morning, Takashi saw Mayumi and talked about the movie he saw with his father. She was very excited to hear about it and wanted to see the movie. Then she asked her father to take her to the theater, but he said he had to see the dentist that day. So, they decided to go to the movie the next day. Her mother and sister said they would like to join them. Her father reserved four movie tickets for his family on the Internet.

The next morning, Mayumi's family went to see the movie. They enjoyed the movie very much. After that, they had lunch and went shopping.

（注）movie theater 映画館　　reserve 予約する

基本料金			
大人	大学生	中・高校生	小学生
1,800 円	1,500 円	1,000 円	800 円

インターネット予約特別料金	
大人 1,800 円を1,500 円に	大学生以下は基本料金と同額

特別料金（大学生以上）	
毎週月曜日・男性	1,100 円
毎週金曜日・女性	1,100 円

タイトル	上映時間		
Stories of Love	9:45〜11:45	15:00〜17:00	18:25〜20:25
The Robot War		14:15〜16:00	16:35〜18:20
The World of Animals	9:35〜11:20	13:35〜15:20	16:35〜18:20
Jack the Rabbit	9:05〜10:40		17:05〜18:40

[問い] 本文の内容から考えて，次の1〜5の英文の（　　）に入る適切なものをア〜エの中から
一つずつ選びなさい。なお，映画のチケットは利用可能な最も安い料金で購入したものとして
計算すること。

1　The movie that Takashi's mother and sister saw was（　　）.
　　ア　Stories of Love　　　イ　The Robot War　　ウ　The World of Animals　　エ　Jack the Rabbit

2　Takashi's family spent（　　）to see the movies.
　　ア　4,900 yen　　　　イ　5,000 yen　　　　ウ　5,400 yen　　　　エ　6,100 yen

3　Takashi waited for his mother and sister for about（　　）before they went home.
　　ア　10 minutes　　　イ　15 minutes　　　ウ　20 minutes　　　エ　30 minutes

4　Mayumi's family spent（　　）to see the movie.
　　ア　4,000 yen　　　　イ　4,800 yen　　　　ウ　5,000 yen　　　　エ　5,400 yen

5　The movie that Mayumi saw was（　　）.
　　ア　Stories of Love　　　イ　The Robot War　　ウ　The World of Animals　　エ　Jack the Rabbit

6　次の文章をよく読んで，後の問いに答えなさい。

About 5,000 years ago, people in Egypt made bread with flour and water. <u>They cooked the bread in the sun.</u> When they traveled, they took bread with them. Other people also learned to make it. Bread became an important food in many places.

It is an old tradition to share bread and other food with friends. This tradition is called "breaking bread." The word "companion" (another word for "friend") tells us about this tradition. *Com* is an old word for "with" and *panis* is an old word for "bread." So a companion is "　1　," a friend.

In every country, family meals are an important tradition. But today people are often busy, and they cannot always eat with their family. Many years ago, the big meal of the day in France was lunch. But today many people are at work or at school at lunch time. So now,　2　. They often sit down at about 8:00 p.m. to eat and talk for an hour or two.

　A　→　B　→　C　

In some countries, there are traditional times for snacks. In England, for example, people ate a snack between breakfast and lunch called "elevenses." At 11:00 a.m. some people still　3　.

In Spanish, "eleven" is *once*. In Chile, there is snack called *once*. People eat bread, meat, and cake. They drink tea or coffee and talk with friends. But people in Chile don't have their *once* at 11:00 in the morning. They have it around 5:00 in the afternoon.

In the past, many families worked on farms. On holidays and at harvest time, they had "feasts." A "feast" is a very large meal people eat with family and friends. Today,　4　, but there are still traditional harvest feasts in the United States and Canada.

（注）　Egypt エジプト　　flour 小麦粉　　　at work 仕事中の　　Spanish スペイン語
　　　　Chile チリ　　　　in the past 昔は　　farm 農場

問1　本文第1段落中の下線部を説明した文として適切なものを，次のア〜ウの中から一つ選びなさい。

　　ア　They made bread which looked like the sun.

　　イ　They used energy from the sun to make bread.

　　ウ　They traveled and made bread in many places.

問2　本文中の空所　1　に入れるのに適切なものを次のア〜ウの中から一つ選びなさい。

　　ア　a person with bread

　　イ　an old tradition with

　　ウ　sharing breakfast with

問3　本文中の空所　2　に入れるのに適切なものを次のア〜ウの中から一つ選びなさい。

　　ア　every family has a big lunch and a small dinner

　　イ　a few families have a small lunch and a big dinner

　　ウ　many families have a small lunch and a big dinner

問4　本文中の一つの段落を構成する空所　A　〜　C　には次の①〜③の英文が入ります。文脈に合うように正しく並べ替えたものを下のア〜ウの中から一つ選びなさい。

　　①　Then they eat a small dinner very late, at about 9:00 p.m.

　　②　So, families can eat a big lunch together.

　　③　In Spain, however, many stores and companies close for lunch.

　　ア　①→②→③　　　　イ　②→③→①　　　　ウ　③→②→①

問5　本文中の空所　3　に入れるのに適切なものを次のア〜ウの中から一つ選びなさい。

　　ア　eat too much and don't walk or play outside

　　イ　stop working and have tea with bread or cake

　　ウ　feel hungry but they work hard until lunch time

問6　本文中の空所　4　に入れるのに適切なものを次のア〜ウの中から一つ選びなさい。

　　ア　fewer families work on farms

　　イ　many people eat three big meals and lots of snacks

　　ウ　many adults and children are often busy at lunch time

問7　本文の内容と合うものを次のア〜ウの中から一つ選びなさい。

　　ア　Families in the U. S. don't have traditional harvest feasts any more.

　　イ　The tradition of family meals is important in every country.

　　ウ　People have traditional times for meals because they work for a long time.

1　次の〔A〕〔B〕それぞれの指示に従って答えなさい。

〔A〕　下の各組のそれぞれの語について，最も強く発音される位置に正しく下線が引かれている
　　　ものを一つずつ選びなさい。

(1)　ア　electri<u>ci</u>ty　　イ　tourna<u>ment</u>　　ウ　e<u>xpe</u>rience　　エ　<u>commu</u>nication

(2)　ア　engi<u>neer</u>　　イ　car<u>pen</u>ter　　ウ　mu<u>si</u>cian　　エ　vol<u>un</u>teer

(3)　ア　medi<u>ci</u>ne　　イ　<u>sci</u>ence　　ウ　prob<u>lem</u>　　エ　res<u>tau</u>rant

(4)　ア　<u>re</u>cycle　　イ　prac<u>tice</u>　　ウ　<u>re</u>spect　　エ　<u>in</u>terview

(5)　ア　<u>ner</u>vous　　イ　qu<u>iet</u>　　ウ　se<u>ri</u>ous　　エ　pop<u>u</u>lar

〔B〕　下のそれぞれの組で，下線部の発音が他と異なる語を一つずつ選びなさい。

(6)　ア　th<u>ou</u>sand　　イ　gr<u>ou</u>p　　ウ　s<u>ou</u>nd　　エ　gr<u>ou</u>nd

(7)　ア　<u>th</u>rough　　イ　<u>th</u>ought　　ウ　<u>th</u>row　　エ　<u>th</u>ough

(8)　ア　d<u>o</u>ne　　イ　l<u>o</u>se　　ウ　n<u>o</u>thing　　エ　<u>o</u>ther

(9)　ア　increa<u>s</u>e　　イ　new<u>s</u>　　ウ　bu<u>s</u>y　　エ　mu<u>s</u>ic

(10)　ア　r<u>ai</u>n　　イ　ch<u>a</u>nge　　ウ　s<u>ai</u>d　　エ　st<u>a</u>dium

2 次の1～5の会話文の(　　　　)に入る適切なものを，それぞれ下の**ア**～**エ**の中から一つずつ選びなさい。

1　A: How often do you go to the library?

　B: (　　　)

　　ア　Yes, I will go there tomorrow.　　**イ**　By bus.

　　ウ　About twice a week.　　**エ**　Yes, I do.

2　A: May I use your bike, Tom?

　B: I'm sorry you can't.

　A: (　　　)

　B: I am going to use it this afternoon.

　　ア　How about you?　　**イ**　Why not?

　　ウ　What was it?　　**エ**　Who is she?

3　A: Excuse me. The 7:20 bus has not come yet. Do you know why?

　B: Today is Sunday. That bus doesn't come on Sunday.

　A: Oh, I see. (　　　)

　B: The earliest one comes at 7:45.

　　ア　When does the next bus come?　　**イ**　Where did the bus go?

　　ウ　Why has the bus already left?　　**エ**　How do you get on the bus?

4　A: Tom, have you finished your homework yet?

　B: Yes, I have. How about you, Ken?

　A: I just finished it now. Shall we check our answers together?

　B: (　　　)

　　ア　Sure, please help me finish it.　　**イ**　Yes, here we are.

　　ウ　No, I haven't finished it yet.　　**エ**　Yes, let's.

5　A: Look at that lady. Do you know who she is?

　B: I don't know.

　A: That's our new math teacher.

　B: (　　　)

　A: I met her in the teachers' room yesterday.

　　ア　What happened to them?　　**イ**　How do you know?

　　ウ　When did you do that?　　**エ**　Who are they?

3　次の文章は，喘息患者でありながらもオリンピック（Olympics）で金メダル（gold medal）を獲得したアメリカ人 Amy Van Dyken に関するものです。これをよく読んで，後の問いに答えなさい。

Amy Van Dyken was a sick child. She had asthma. People with asthma sometimes can't breathe well. When Amy was a child, she went to the hospital many times and she couldn't do the things other children could do. Her doctor ｱbelieved that swimming was good for asthma. （　1　）Amy began swimming and she liked it. In the beginning, Amy couldn't ｲswim（　2　）and she was always the last when she took part in races. It was very hard for her, but she （　3　）gave up trying. After a few years she could swim faster. When she was 13, she started to（　4　）races. When she was in high school and college, she was one of the fastest swimmers in the U.S.

When the Olympics ｳarrived in 1996, Amy took part in five events and won four gold medals! She was the first American woman to ｴwin four gold medals in one Olympics. In the next Olympics in 2000 she won two（　5　）gold medals.

In June 2014, Amy was ｵinjured in an accident which damaged her spinal cord. After the accident, she lost feeling in her legs. Many people thought that Amy would not be able to ｶwalk again. However, she did not give up. In August 2014, she was able to walk with a walker.

Amy's story now（　6　）many people, especially people with asthma or with injured spinal cords.

（注） asthma 喘息　　　　breathe 呼吸する　　　race レース，競争　　　accident 事故
　　　damage 損傷を与える　spinal cord 脊髄　　　walker 歩行器

問1　本文中の（　1　）～（　6　）に入れるのに適切なものを，次のア～エの中から一つずつ選びなさい。

（ 1 ）	ア	while	イ	though	ウ	so	エ	if
（ 2 ）	ア	very	イ	fast	ウ	little	エ	most
（ 3 ）	ア	always	イ	never	ウ	often	エ	usually
（ 4 ）	ア	break	イ	follow	ウ	lose	エ	win
（ 5 ）	ア	more	イ	some	ウ	much	エ	any
（ 6 ）	ア	agrees	イ	encourages	ウ	stands	エ	leaves

問2　次の1と2が表している語を，本文中の下線部ア～カからそれぞれ一つずつ選びなさい。

1　move by putting one foot in front of the other on the ground

2　think that something is true

4 次の1～5の会話文の（　　）内の語句を並べ替え，それぞれの文を完成しなさい。解答は，（　　）内において**3番目**と**5番目**にくるものの記号を選びなさい。なお，文頭にくる語も小文字で書かれています。

1　A: Let's go to see a movie next Saturday.

　　B: I'm sorry I can't. My mother has to go to work and I（ア care　イ have　ウ of　エ take　オ to　カ will）my little sister.

2　A: The concert was wonderful. Did you like the songs?

　　B: Yes, I liked them very much.（ア me　イ inviting　ウ for　エ thank　オ to　カ you）the concert.

　　A: I am happy you could come with us.

3　A: How can I get to the airport?

　　B: I think going by bus is the fastest, but you（ア be　イ careful　ウ get　エ on　オ should　カ to）the right bus.

4　A: I visited Hokkaido with my family this summer. We really enjoyed our trip.

　　B: I（ア pictures　イ see　ウ the　エ to　オ want　カ you）took there.

5　A: （ア about　イ buying　ウ for　エ how　オ shirt　カ this）Mom's birthday? Do you think she'll like it?

　　B: I'm sure she will.

　　A: OK, let's get it.

5　次の文章を，図を見ながらよく読んで，後の問いに答えなさい。なお，登場人物は全員が一定
速度の徒歩で移動し，目的地までは必ず最短コースを取るものとする。

Takashi, Kenji, Sayuri and Mayumi are classmates at Sakura Junior High School.

Takashi has a brother who goes to Hibari Elementary School. Takashi leaves home for school together with his brother every morning because his brother's school is on the way to Takashi's school. Takashi walks for twenty minutes, and his brother walks for fifteen minutes to go to school.

Kenji usually leaves home for school at seven thirty-five, and arrives at seven fifty.

Sayuri has a sister who goes to the same school as Takashi's brother. Her sister walks straight from their house to her school, and it takes twenty minutes.

Mayumi usually leaves home for school at seven thirty and she walks for the same number of minutes as Takashi.

One Sunday, Takashi went to Kenji's house to play a new video game with him. He left his house at ten o'clock. At one o'clock in the afternoon, the two boys left Kenji's house because they had a plan to play tennis with Mayumi and Sayuri at their school. The two girls came from each of their own homes. When the boys arrived at the school, the two girls also arrived just at the same time.

　下の図は，上の文章に関する略図で，直線（実線）は道路を表し，点 A，B，C，D は登場人物の
住む家の位置を示す。なお，AC と BD は垂直に交わっているものとする。

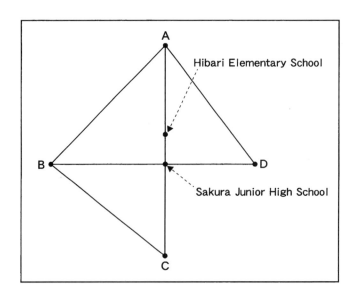

［問い］ 本文の内容から考えて，次の1〜5の英文の（　　）に入る適切なものを**ア**〜**エ**の中から
それぞれ一つずつ選びなさい。

1　Takashi's house is（　　）on the map.

　　ア　A　　　　　　　　**イ**　B　　　　　　　**ウ**　C　　　　　　　**エ**　D

2　Sayuri's house is（　　）on the map.

　　ア　A　　　　　　　　**イ**　B　　　　　　　**ウ**　C　　　　　　　**エ**　D

3　If Sayuri leaves home for school at 7：20, she arrives at（　　）.

　　ア　7：30　　　　　　**イ**　7：35　　　　　**ウ**　7：40　　　　　**エ**　7：45

4　When Takashi went to Kenji's house, he arrived at（　　）.

　　ア　10：15　　　　　　**イ**　10：20　　　　　**ウ**　10：25　　　　　**エ**　10：30

5　Mayumi left home at（　　）to play tennis with her friends.

　　ア　12：55　　　　　　**イ**　13：00　　　　　**ウ**　13：15　　　　　**エ**　13：20

6　以下は，"The Moving Stones" という題名の文章です。これをよく読んで，後の問いに答えなさい。

Lots of American people watch birds. That's easy to understand. Birds are beautiful. They do interesting things. However, ⬚1⬚ in America. That's easy to understand, too. Stones don't do interesting things. They just lie there. Watch one for a while, and you will find it boring.

But ⬚2⬚ for one group of stones in the California desert. The stones did a strange thing. They didn't just lie there, but ⬚3⬚.

Once there were lakes in the desert. The lakes dried up long ago. Now the land is hard and flat, and the stones lie there.

No one thinks that stones can move by themselves, but these stones actually have long tracks. Lots of people have seen the tracks.

No one knew why the stones moved. Were they looking for something? Were they playing? Most people didn't think the stones moved because they wanted to move. In winter, there is a little ice in the desert. Some people thought that the ice moved the stones.

Two scientists didn't think it was just the ice. So, in 1972, ⬚4⬚. First, they chose thirty stones that had tracks behind them and wrote names on the stones. One was Mary Ann. One was Ruth. A large stone was named Karen. Then they put a metal stake into the ground by each stone. It showed ⬚5⬚. They watched the stones for seven years. During that time, several stones moved away from their stakes. A stone named Nancy moved 201 meters, but Karen was still at the same place.

Now the scientists know why the stones move. It is because of the wind. ⬚A⬚ → ⬚B⬚ → ⬚C⬚ The stone moves while the wind blows. When the wind stops, the stone stops. This is the fact the scientists have found.

(注) California desert カリフォルニアの砂漠地帯　　　dry up 干上がる　　　flat 平らな
track 通った跡　　　metal stake 金属の杭（くい）

問1　本文中の空所　| 1 |　に入れるのに適切なものを次の**ア～ウ**の中から一つ選びなさい。

　ア　stone watching is more popular than bird watching

　イ　bird watching is just as popular as stone watching

　ウ　few people watch stones

問2　本文中の空所　| 2 |　に入れるのに適切なものを次の**ア～ウ**の中から一つ選びなさい。

　ア　things have changed

　イ　the environment has never changed

　ウ　the Internet has made life easier

問3　本文中の空所　| 3 |　に入れるのに適切なものを次の**ア～ウ**の中から一つ選びなさい。

　ア　they all disappeared from the desert

　イ　they moved by themselves

　ウ　they were produced by the scientists

問4　本文中の空所　| 4 |　に入れるのに適切なものを次の**ア～ウ**の中から一つ選びなさい。

　ア　they started watching the stones

　イ　they broke the stones into pieces

　ウ　they tried to look for other deserts

問5　本文中の空所　| 5 |　に入れるのに適切なものを次の**ア～ウ**の中から一つ選びなさい。

　ア　how the stones were growing

　イ　where the scientists found the stone

　ウ　when the ice was made

問6　本文中の空所　| A |　～　| C |　には次の①～③の英文が入ります。文脈に合うように正しく並べ替えたものを下の**ア～ウ**の中から一つ選びなさい。

　①　The water on the ground becomes ice during the cold winter nights.

　②　Then a strong wind moves the stone on the ice.

　③　Sometimes it rains on the ground.

　ア　①→②→③　　　　　**イ**　②→③→①　　　　　**ウ**　③→①→②

問7　本文の内容と合うものを次の**ア～ウ**の中から一つ選びなさい。

　ア　The scientists first realized that the stones moved in the 21st century.

　イ　From 1972 to 1979, a stone named Karen moved 201 meters.

　ウ　People thought that the stones moved because they saw the tracks made by the stones.

1　次の〔A〕〔B〕それぞれの指示に従って答えなさい。

〔A〕　下の各組のそれぞれの語について，最も強く発音される位置に正しく下線が引かれているものを一つずつ選びなさい。

(1)　ア　a<u>gree</u>　　　イ　be<u>lieve</u>　　　ウ　<u>con</u>tinue　　　エ　<u>de</u>cide

(2)　ア　<u>a</u>mong　　　イ　be<u>hind</u>　　　ウ　be<u>tween</u>　　　エ　dur<u>ing</u>

(3)　ア　hos<u>pi</u>tal　　　イ　in<u>flu</u>ence　　　ウ　is<u>land</u>　　　エ　mu<u>se</u>um

(4)　ア　<u>e</u>nergy　　　イ　lan<u>guage</u>　　　ウ　mes<u>sage</u>　　　エ　pro<u>gram</u>

(5)　ア　<u>for</u>eign　　　イ　inter<u>na</u>tional　　　ウ　ne<u>ces</u>sary　　　エ　tra<u>di</u>tional

〔B〕　下のそれぞれの組で，下線部の発音が他と異なる語を一つずつ選びなさい。

(6)　ア　alr<u>ea</u>dy　　　イ　h<u>ea</u>d　　　ウ　l<u>ea</u>ve　　　エ　s<u>ai</u>d

(7)　ア　aftern<u>oo</u>n　　　イ　ch<u>oo</u>se　　　ウ　f<u>oo</u>d　　　エ　w<u>oo</u>d

(8)　ア　f<u>a</u>vorite　　　イ　l<u>a</u>ter　　　ウ　pr<u>a</u>ctice　　　エ　r<u>ai</u>se

(9)　ア　d<u>ear</u>　　　イ　<u>ear</u>ly　　　ウ　h<u>ear</u>　　　エ　y<u>ear</u>

(10)　ア　<u>ch</u>ildren　　　イ　ma<u>ch</u>ine　　　ウ　<u>ch</u>arity　　　エ　tou<u>ch</u>

2　次の1～5の会話文の（　　　　）に入る適切なものを，それぞれ下の**ア～エ**の中から一つず
つ選びなさい。

1　A: Is this your ticket? I found this on the floor by your seat.

B: （　　　） Thank you very much.

ア　No, I can't find my seat.　　　　　イ　You've lost your ticket.

ウ　I guess it's mine, then.　　　　　エ　No, it's difficult to find one.

2　A: Take this medicine before you go to bed.

B: （　　　）

A: Don't do that. It will make you sleepy.

ア　Do you sleep in the bed?　　　　　イ　Do you want to go to bed now?

ウ　Can I take care of you?　　　　　エ　Can I take it in the morning?

3　A: When you go to a restaurant and you have a choice, which do you choose, rice or bread?

B: （　　　）, so if I go out, I choose bread.

A: Me, too. I love bread.

ア　You have no choice　　　　　イ　It has been closed

ウ　I always eat rice at home　　　　　エ　You hate both of them

4　A: What did you eat for breakfast today?

B: （　　　）

A: Why not?

B: I got up late.

ア　I had breakfast, too.　　　　　イ　I want to eat something.

ウ　I have nothing to do.　　　　　エ　I ate nothing this morning.

5　A: May I speak to Mr. John Green, please?

B: Oh, is that you, Fred?

A: Yes...

B: （　　　） How have you been, Fred?

ア　It's me!　　　　　イ　It's mine!

ウ　There she is!　　　　　エ　Here it is!

3 次の文章は，アフリカの太鼓(drum)に関するものです。これをよく読んで，後の問いに答えなさい。

Drums have played a big part in the music of people all over the world. But in many parts of Africa, drums have had a more important (1).

For many years, parts of Africa had few good roads. There were few telephones and TVs and there was no e-mail. Then, how did people send messages to each other? How did they get their news? They used drums!

These drums are called "talking drums." They are used by the Yoruba people of Nigeria. These drums are not able to talk in English, (2) they can talk in Yoruba and some other languages.

In English you say "Hello!" or "How are you?" You just say the words any way you like. But you can't do that in Yoruba. You must be (3) how you say each word. This is because the same word may have two or more meanings. The meaning depends on how (4) your voice is as you say the word.

When people speak Yoruba, their voices go up and down. They sound like they are singing, but of course they don't really sing. They are talking.

After years of (5) a drum player can "talk" on a drum because he hits the drum in different ways to make high or low notes. The notes and rhythm of the drum then match the sounds of the language. Like this, the Yoruba people can understand every word that the drum "(6)."

（注）Yoruba　ヨルバ族（の），ヨルバ語　　　Nigeria　ナイジェリア
　　　depend on～　～によって決まる　　　voice　声　　　　　　　　note　音調
　　　rhythm　リズム　　　　　　　　　　　match ～　～に合う

問1　本文中の（ 1 ）～（ 6 ）に入れるのに適切なものを，それぞれア～エの中から一つずつ選びなさい。

(1)	ア dream	イ job	ウ care	エ plan
(2)	ア so	イ then	ウ but	エ and
(3)	ア afraid	イ excited	ウ favorite	エ careful
(4)	ア low or high	イ short or long	ウ little or much	エ difficult or easy
(5)	ア war	イ peace	ウ harvest	エ practice
(6)	ア listens	イ listened	ウ speaks	エ spoken

問2　次の1と2が説明しているものを，本文中の下線ア～カからそれぞれ一つずつ選びなさい。

1　a system of communication by written or spoken words

2　information about something that happened a short time ago

4 次の1～5の会話文の（　　）内の語句を並べ替え，それぞれの文を完成しなさい。解答は，（　　）内において**3番目**と**5番目**にくるものの記号を選びなさい。

1　A: How many（ア does　イ fly　ウ hours　エ it　オ take　カ to ）to Australia?

　　B: About eight hours.

2　A: I have something important to ask you.

　　B: What is it?

　　A: Please（ア about　イ anyone　ウ don't　エ meeting　オ our　カ tell ）today.

　　B: Sure, it's just between the two of us.

3　A: Have you ever seen old Japanese money used a hundred years ago?

　　B: No, I（ア don't　イ it　ウ know　エ like　オ looks　カ what ）.

　　A: I have some. Look.

　　B: Oh, it's interesting.

4　A: Where did you go last summer?

　　B: Can you guess? I went（ア famous　イ most　ウ of　エ one　オ the　カ to ）places in
　　　the world.

　　A: Well, did you go to Hawaii?

　　B: No, I went to Paris!

5　A: I think more people speak English than any other language in the world. Is that right?

　　B: No, it isn't. Chinese is spoken by the largest number of people.

　　A: So, English（ア isn't　イ language　ウ should　エ study　オ the only　カ we ）then.

　　B: You're right.

5   次の文章および下の表をよく読んで，後の問いに答えなさい。

　　Takashi is a student of Sakura Junior High School.　He is in the third grade.　Mayumi is Takashi's classmate.　She is one of the twenty girls in her class.　Sakura Junior High School has only one third grade class, and there are thirty-six students in the class.

　　One day, the third grade students of Sakura Junior High School went to Kyoto on a school trip.　Three teachers went with the students.　They took a Shinkansen train and arrived at Kyoto Station at 9 : 00.

　　After arriving at Kyoto Station, the students broke into groups to travel around the city by taxi.　Before the students came, each group made a plan to visit at least three places in the city of Kyoto on the first day.　Each taxi could carry four passengers.　The teachers went around the city by bus.

　　Takashi's group visited Kinkaku-ji first.　At the next place, they met Mayumi's group that came from Ginkaku-ji.　They had lunch together.

　　At 17 : 30, all the students and the teachers gathered at the hotel.　The rooms for the boys were on the second floor, and the rooms for the girls were on the third floor.　Each room for the students had three beds and each room for the teachers had one bed.

（注）break into ～　～に分かれる　　at least　少なくとも，最小限　　passenger　乗客
　　　　gather　集合する

桜中学校修学旅行 見学地滞在時間				
	金閣寺	銀閣寺	清水寺	二条城
A 班	9:30 − 11:30	12:00 − 13:00	15:30 − 17:00	13:30 − 15:00
B 班	9:30 − 11:30	12:00 − 13:00	13:30 − 15:00	15:30 − 17:00
C 班	13:00 − 15:00		9:30 − 12:30	15:30 − 17:00
D 班	9:30 − 11:00	16:00 − 17:00	11:30 − 13:30	14:00 − 15:30
E 班	15:00 − 17:00	9:30 − 11:00	11:30 − 14:30	
⋮	⋮	⋮	⋮	⋮
⋮	⋮	⋮	⋮	⋮

[問い]　本文の内容から考えて，次の 1 ～ 5 の英文の（　　）に入る適切なものをア～エの中か
　　　らそれぞれ一つずつ選びなさい。

1　There are （　　） boys in Takashi's class.
　　ア　16　　　　　　　イ　20　　　　　　　ウ　36　　　　　　　エ　40

2　The students of Sakura Junior High School used at least （　　） taxis.
　　ア　9　　　　　　　　イ　10　　　　　　　ウ　11　　　　　　　エ　12

3　Takashi was in group （　　）.
　　ア　A　　　　　　　　イ　B　　　　　　　　ウ　C　　　　　　　　エ　D

4　Mayumi had lunch at （　　）.
　　ア　Kinkaku-ji　　イ　Ginkaku-ji　　ウ　Kiyomizu-dera　　エ　Nijo-jo

5　The students and teachers of Sakura Junior High School needed at least （　　） hotel rooms.
　　ア　12　　　　　　　イ　13　　　　　　　ウ　15　　　　　　　エ　16

6 次の文章は，台風(typhoon)やハリケーン(hurricane)などの嵐(storm)に関するものです。
これをよく読んで，後の問いに答えなさい。

　　In different parts of the world, big storms are named in different ways. They are called
"typhoons" in Japan and they ⬚ 1 ⬚ . However, in the United States, big storms are called
"hurricanes," and they have names like "William" or "Emily." In 2012, Hurricane Sandy
damaged a lot of cities in the United States. This storm caused 125 billion dollars in damage.
Why was it named "Sandy"?

　　The naming of hurricanes started almost two hundred years ago. The first was in 1825
when Hurricane Santa Ana hit Puerto Rico. Later, the U.S. military began to use women's
names to remember hurricanes more easily. In 1953, the American National Hurricane Center
started naming hurricanes. The names were used in news reports so ⬚ 2 ⬚ .

　　Today, both men's and women's names are kept on six different lists for Atlantic
hurricanes. One list is used each year. The first storm name begins with the letter "A," the
first letter of the English alphabet. The second storm gets a name that starts with "B," the
second letter of the English alphabet, and so on. But names that start with the letters Q, U, X,
Y, and Z are not on the lists. After all six lists are used, they are reused from the beginning.
However, ⬚ 3 ⬚ , so their names are never used for hurricanes again.

　　Seven years before Hurricane Sandy hit a lot of cities, much of the city of New Orleans was
damaged by Hurricane Katrina. Hurricane Katrina caused 50 billion dollars in damage. Now a
lot of Americans remember those two hurricanes because they were terrible.

　　Some hurricanes come near land but then turn back out to sea without causing any
damage. When that happens, people will sometimes name their children after that
storm ⬚ 4 ⬚ .

　　(注) damage　損害（を与える）　　　cause 〜 dollars in damage　〜ドルの損害をもたらす
　　　　billion　10億　　　　　　　　　Puerto Rico　プエルトリコ
　　　　the U.S. military　アメリカ軍　　Atlantic　大西洋の
　　　　letter　文字　　　　　　　　　　alphabet　アルファベット
　　　　New Orleans　ニューオーリンズ
　　　　name 〜 after …　…にちなんで 〜に名前をつける

問1　本文中の空所 [1] に入れるのに適切なものを次の**ア〜ウ**の中から一つ選びなさい。

　　ア　are built in the same size　　**イ**　are broken by people　　**ウ**　are given numbers

問2　本文中の空所 [2] に入れるのに適切なものを次の**ア〜ウ**の中から一つ選びなさい。

　　ア　people could remember the storms easily

　　イ　there were more cities damaged by hurricanes

　　ウ　all the cities in America had their own lists

問3　本文中の空所 [3] に入れるのに適切なものを次の**ア〜ウ**の中から一つ選びなさい。

　　ア　the U.S. military uses only women's names for storms

　　イ　some storms hit a lot of cities and cause a lot of damage

　　ウ　the lists are difficult to read in other languages

問4　本文中の空所 [4] に入れるのに適切なものを次の**ア〜ウ**の中から一つ選びなさい。

　　ア　because it is not good for their children

　　イ　if it causes a lot of damage

　　ウ　as a symbol of good luck

問5　本文中の Hurricane Katrina を表している英文を次の**ア〜ウ**の中から一つ選びなさい。

　　ア　It hit the city of New Orleans and caused 125 billion dollars in damage.

　　イ　It was the 11th hurricane of 2005 and it damaged the city of New Orleans.

　　ウ　It was named by people in New Orleans because they wanted to remember it.

問6　Atlantic hurricane に "Walter" という名前が付けられた場合，それはその年に発生した何番目のハリケーンだと考えられるか。本文の内容をもとに推測し，適切なものを次の**ア〜ウ**の中から一つ選びなさい。

　　ア　19 番目　　　　　　　　　**イ**　21 番目　　　　　　　　　**ウ**　23 番目

問7　本文の内容と合うものを次の**ア〜ウ**の中から一つ選びなさい。

　　ア　Santa Ana was a storm that hit Puerto Rico in the 20th century.

　　イ　People in the United States like to name their cities after terrible hurricanes.

　　ウ　Hurricane Sandy in 2012 caused greater damage than Hurricane Katrina.

1　次の〔A〕〔B〕それぞれの指示に従って答えなさい。

〔A〕　下の各組のそれぞれの語について，最も強く発音される位置に正しく下線が引かれている
　　　ものを一つずつ選びなさい。

(1)　ア　or<u>ange</u>　　　　イ　<u>i</u>dea　　　　ウ　c<u>a</u>mera　　　　エ　uni<u>form</u>

(2)　ア　<u>al</u>ready　　　　イ　<u>with</u>out　　　　ウ　<u>news</u>paper　　　　エ　<u>um</u>brella

(3)　ア　sud<u>den</u>ly　　　　イ　mu<u>si</u>cian　　　　ウ　c<u>on</u>venient　　　　エ　tra<u>di</u>tional

(4)　ア　sc<u>i</u>entist　　　　イ　pro<u>gram</u>　　　　ウ　caf<u>e</u>teria　　　　エ　ch<u>o</u>colate

〔B〕　下のそれぞれの組で，下線部の発音が他と異なる語を一つずつ選びなさい。

(5)　ア　<u>ear</u>th　　　　イ　p<u>ar</u>k　　　　ウ　h<u>ear</u>t　　　　エ　p<u>ar</u>ty

(6)　ア　h<u>o</u>me　　　　イ　c<u>oa</u>t　　　　ウ　b<u>oa</u>t　　　　エ　c<u>au</u>ght

(7)　ア　chang<u>ed</u>　　　　イ　watch<u>ed</u>　　　　ウ　clean<u>ed</u>　　　　エ　receiv<u>ed</u>

(8)　ア　<u>th</u>rough　　　　イ　ba<u>th</u>　　　　ウ　wea<u>th</u>er　　　　エ　any<u>th</u>ing

2 次の１～５の会話文の（　　　）に入る適切なものを，それぞれ下のア～エの中から一つずつ選びなさい。

1　A: It's getting dark. （　　　）
　　B: No, I can't. I'm too tired.

　　　　ア　Shall we walk faster?　　　　　　イ　What can I do for you?
　　　　ウ　How have you been?　　　　　　　エ　What's the matter?

2　A: I heard you don't like coffee.
　　B: （　　　）
　　A: Oh? I do, too.

　　　　ア　Yes, I do. I don't like it very much.　イ　Well, I like it when it has milk.
　　　　ウ　No, thank you.　　　　　　　　　　エ　I've never had it before.

3　A: Shall we play soccer this afternoon?
　　B: The weather report says it's going to rain.
　　A: Then let's play volleyball in the gym.
　　B: （　　　）

　　　　ア　Okay. Let's go to the soccer field.　イ　Yes, let's. I'll play soccer.
　　　　ウ　Me, too. I like it very much.　　　エ　I'm sorry. I have many things to do.

4　A: I heard that you play the guitar very well.
　　B: Thanks. You're very kind to say so.
　　A: （　　　）
　　B: Almost every day.

　　　　ア　How long have you played the guitar?　イ　How often do you practice the guitar?
　　　　ウ　How many guitars do you have?　　　　エ　How did you learn to play the guitar?

5　A: You didn't come to school yesterday. （　　　）
　　B: I had a headache.
　　A: Are you all right now?
　　B: Yes. Thank you.

　　　　ア　What did you have for lunch?　　　イ　Where did you come from?
　　　　ウ　What was wrong with you?　　　　エ　Where would you like to go?

3 次の文章中の（ 1 ）～（ 6 ）に入る適切なものを，それぞれ下の**ア**～**エ**の中から一つずつ選びなさい。

Ms. Nishizaki Kiku was born in Saitama in 1912. She was a very active girl. When she was only four, she went up to the roof of her house alone. Her parents were very （ 1 ）, but she looked very happy on the roof.

In 1929, she became a teacher at an elementary school in her village. She enjoyed （ 2 ） at school. One day, she went to the airport, and she touched a plane for the first time in her life. A few months later, she got on a plane and she became more interested （ 3 ） flying than teaching.

In 1931, she entered a pilots' school. Two years later, she became the first woman pilot in Japan. One day, her plane left the airport in Aichi for Saitama. It was a long flight and it （ 4 ） about seven hours. A lot of people were waiting for her. She was so happy to see some of her students among those people.

She was the first Japanese woman pilot （ 5 ） to other countries. In 1934, when she was flying to China, she had engine trouble and had to land on a river bank at night.

In 1935, she won a prize as the best pilot in the world. "When I heard the good news, I couldn't believe my ears," she said. "I like this prize the best （ 6 ） all, because Charles Lindbergh also won the same prize."

Ms. Nishizaki always said, "Have a dream. Work hard for it, and your dream will come true."

（注）	active 活発な	pilot パイロット	engine エンジン
	land 着陸する	bank 土手	prize 賞
	Charles Lindbergh	チャールズ・リンドバーグ（単独での大西洋無着陸横断飛行を世界	
		で初めて行った人）	

（ 1 ）	**ア** surprise	**イ** surprising	**ウ** surprised	**エ** to surprise
（ 2 ）	**ア** teach	**イ** teaching	**ウ** taught	**エ** to teach
（ 3 ）	**ア** at	**イ** in	**ウ** of	**エ** with
（ 4 ）	**ア** brought	**イ** came	**ウ** made	**エ** took
（ 5 ）	**ア** flew	**イ** flying	**ウ** flown	**エ** to fly
（ 6 ）	**ア** at	**イ** for	**ウ** of	**エ** than

4 次の 1 ～ 5 の会話文の( )内の語を並べ替え，それぞれの文を完成しなさい。解答は，( )内において **3番目** と **5番目** にくるものの記号を選びなさい。

1 A: What are you reading?

B: I'm reading *Botchan*.

A: Oh, I know it. It is (ア famous　イ of　ウ one　エ stories　オ the　カ written) by Natsume Soseki.

B: Yes, it is.

2 A: How long have you used this bag?

B: I've (ア I　イ it　ウ since　エ started　オ used　カ working) five years ago.

3 A: Do you want to know about the history of computers?

B: Yes, I do. Please tell me.

A: A scientist wanted to (ア easier　イ father's　ウ for　エ his　オ make　カ work) him.

4 A: It's so hot in here. Are you OK?

B: I'm very thirsty. Do you know (ア buy　イ can　ウ cold　エ I　オ something　カ where) to drink?

A: How about going to the restaurant across the street?

B: That's a good idea.

5 A: Why are you so sad?

B: I (ア broke　イ cup　ウ gave　エ me　オ the　カ Tom) for my birthday.

5　次の〔A〕〔B〕の文章をよく読んで，後の問題に答えなさい。

〔A〕

　　One afternoon, Akiko's mother bought a cake and some bottles of juice because it was Akiko's birthday.　The cake was very large, so her mother cut the cake in half.　She put one half in the refrigerator.　Akiko and her parents shared the other half.　Her mother cut the cake into three pieces.　The size of each piece was the same.　Just as they started to eat the cake, her father received a phone call and had to go to his office.　So he could not eat any of the cake.　Her mother put the cake that her father left into the refrigerator.　After that, Akiko and her mother each drank half a bottle of juice.

　　That evening, Akiko's friends — Yumiko, Tomoko, and Saori — came to her house.　Akiko asked her mother to serve the cake in the refrigerator.　Her mother took all the cake out of the refrigerator, and cut the cake for Akiko, her friends, and herself.　Everyone had the same amount of cake.　Akiko's friends drank the juice that her mother bought.　But Akiko and her mother drank coffee without sugar.

〔B〕

　　The cake which Akiko's mother bought was 1500 g, and there was 500 ml in each bottle of juice.　There was 10 g of sugar in each 100 g piece of cake.　There was 10 g of sugar in every 100 ml of juice.

　　(注)　half　半分　　　　refrigerator　冷蔵庫　　　　serve　（料理などを）出す
　　　　　amount　量　　　sugar　砂糖

〔問題〕　本文の内容から考えて，次の１〜５の英文の（　　　）に入る適切なものをア〜エの中からそれぞれ一つずつ選びなさい。

1　The cake Akiko's mother bought had (　　　) of sugar in it.
　　ア　10 g　　　　　　イ　25 g　　　　　　ウ　100 g　　　　　エ　150 g
2　The piece of cake Akiko's father couldn't eat was (　　　).
　　ア　200 g　　　　　イ　250 g　　　　　ウ　300 g　　　　　エ　350 g
3　The juice Akiko drank had (　　　) of sugar.
　　ア　10 g　　　　　　イ　20 g　　　　　　ウ　25 g　　　　　　エ　50 g
4　Each of Akiko's friends ate (　　　) of cake.
　　ア　150 g　　　　　イ　175 g　　　　　ウ　200 g　　　　　エ　250 g
5　There was (　　　) of sugar in the cake and juice Akiko had on her birthday.
　　ア　50 g　　　　　　イ　70 g　　　　　　ウ　100 g　　　　　エ　125 g

〔 計 算 用 紙 〕

6 　次の文章をよく読み，その下の地図を参考にして，後の問いに答えなさい。

　　It's 3 p.m. in New York now. What time is it in Los Angeles? It's noon. Why? It's because of time zones. For example, students in New York go to school at 8 a.m. and the sun is up. However, students in Los Angeles have to go to school 　1　 if they go at the same time. Why? Because 　2　 . So, the sun rises every morning and sets every evening. The parts of the earth which face the sun have day and the other parts have night. This changes during the 24 hours of each day.

　　We didn't always have time zones. For thousands of years, people used sun clocks, water clocks and other kinds of clocks that showed what time of day it was, but no one knew about minutes or hours. A few hundred years ago, clocks and watches were invented, but no one understood that 　3　 .

　　In 1879, a man named Sandford Fleming divided the world into 24 time zones, and the United States was divided into four time zones. Each time zone is one hour behind the time zone to its east. So, when it's 8 a.m. in Los Angeles, it's 　4　 in New York.

　　The map dividing the U.S. into the four time zones doesn't always go straight down state lines. Some states are in two different time zones. So, when you take a trip through these states, you may see clocks that show two different times. What does all this mean? It means that 　5　 when you travel in the United States!

　　(注)　Los Angeles　ロサンゼルス　　　face　～の方を向いている　　　invent　発明する
　　　　　divide　分割する　　　　　　　　behind　遅れて　　　　　　　　east　東
　　　　　state　州

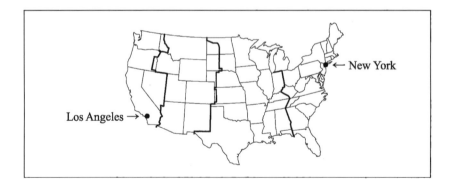

問 1 本文中の空所 ⎡ 1 ⎤ に入れるのに適切なものを次の**ア**～**ウ**の中から一つ選びなさい。

　　ア before the sun rises　　**イ** before the sun sets　　**ウ** at noon

問 2 本文中の空所 ⎡ 2 ⎤ に入れるのに適切なものを次の**ア**～**ウ**の中から一つ選びなさい。

　　ア the sun is turning　　　　　　**イ** the earth is turning

　　ウ the moon goes around the earth

問 3 本文中の空所 ⎡ 3 ⎤ に入れるのに適切なものを次の**ア**～**ウ**の中から一つ選びなさい。

　　ア they couldn't do anything without a map

　　イ the sun goes around the earth

　　ウ time zones were needed

問 4 本文中の空所 ⎡ 4 ⎤ に入れるのに適切なものを次の**ア**～**ウ**の中から一つ選びなさい。

　　ア 5 a.m.　　　　　　**イ** 11 a.m.　　　　　　**ウ** noon

問 5 本文中の空所 ⎡ 5 ⎤ に入れるのに適切なものを次の**ア**～**ウ**の中から一つ選びなさい。

　　ア you can visit everywhere in the world

　　イ you should have two different maps

　　ウ you will need to check the local time

問 6 本文中の "time zone" の説明として適切なものを次の**ア**～**ウ**の中から一つ選びなさい。

　　ア A time zone is the line dividing the countries of the world.

　　イ A time zone is one of the 24 areas that the world is divided into.

　　ウ A time zone was invented because people had state lines in the U.S.

問 7 本文の内容と合うものを次の**ア**～**ウ**の中から一つ選びなさい。

　　ア Sun clocks and water clocks were invented to tell time using hours and minutes.

　　イ Thousands of years ago, everyone thought that each day had 24 hours.

　　ウ There are states in the U.S. that have different times.

1 次の(1)～(5)の各組の英文において，アとイの文中の（　　　）に共通する適切な1語を入れなさい。なお，その語は解答欄のマス目の数と同じ文字数の語です。解答欄に書かれた1文字目に続けて正しくつづりなさい。

(1) ア An (e　　　) is a person who designs or builds things like roads, buildings, and machines.

イ My father is working as an (e　　　) in a computer company.

(2) ア I'm late because I (m　　　) the train this morning.

イ Where have you been? I (m　　　) you very much.

(3) ア Burning plastic bags causes (g　　　) warming.

イ People gathered from many countries to talk about the problems of the (g　　　) environment.

(4) ア April is the (f　　　) month of the year.

イ May the (f　　　) is a holiday called "*Midori no Hi*" in Japan.

(5) ア I use my computer every day to look for (i　　　) on the Internet.

イ Something strange happened last night. Please tell me some (i　　　) about it.

2 次の1～5の会話文の（　　）に入る適切なものを，それぞれ下のア～エの中から一つずつ選び，記号で答えなさい。

1　A: Let's watch a different TV program.
　　B: Why? It's a good game.
　　A: (　　)
　　B: Don't worry, you soon will.

　　　ア　I think it's exciting.　　　　　イ　I think you're right.
　　　ウ　I don't understand the rules.　エ　I'm sorry, but I can't.

2　A: How do you like it here in Japan, Mary?
　　B: Oh, I'm having a very good time.
　　A: (　　)
　　B: I will be here for another two weeks.

　　　ア　How do you do?
　　　イ　How have you been?
　　　ウ　How many times have you been here?
　　　エ　How long are you going to stay?

3　A: Could you sit here, please?
　　B: Sure. Thank you.
　　A: (　　)
　　B: Well, I'd like to keep the top long, but I'd like the back and sides nice and short.

　　　ア　How would you like your hair today?
　　　イ　Does your tooth still hurt?
　　　ウ　How long do you want to stay?
　　　エ　Which chair do you like?

4　A: We're having a party on Saturday night. Can you come?
　　B: (　　)
　　A: Oh, well, maybe next time!

　　　ア　Yes, of course I can come.　　イ　I'm busy this weekend.
　　　ウ　Why not?　　　　　　　　　　エ　I think it's a very good idea.

5　A: Hello.
　　B: Hello. Could I speak to Mr. Brown, please?
　　A: I'm sorry. He's not here right now. (　　)
　　B: Sure. That'll be fine.

　　　ア　Shall I ask him to call you back?　イ　Where are you calling from?
　　　ウ　What's the matter with you?　　　エ　Can I leave a message?

3 以下は，「ロボット義足」を作った Hugh Herr（ヒュー・ハー）さんへのインタビューです。
（ 1 ）～（ 5 ）に入る適切なものを，それぞれ下のア～エの中から一つずつ選び，記号で
答えなさい。

Interviewer: Tonight, we are going to speak to Hugh Herr. Hi, Hugh. You lost your legs in
an accident. Could you tell me how it（ 1 ）?

Hugh Herr: Sure. I was climbing Mt. Washington in 1982. Suddenly the weather became
really bad and it started snowing. I couldn't see anything and got lost. It was
almost −30℃. I spent four days on the mountain. I didn't have any food or
equipment. When I was found, I was very sick. I couldn't move my legs
（ 2 ）the cold. I was taken to a hospital and spent two months there. While
I was there, the doctors（ 3 ）both of my legs.

Interviewer: Oh, I see. But you wanted to continue mountain climbing.

Hugh Herr: That's right. So I decided to make some new legs for（ 4 ）.

Interviewer: And you built these great new legs, didn't you?

Hugh Herr: Yes, I did. In my tests, these legs really（ 5 ）well. And they are much
more powerful than climbing shoes!

Interviewer: That's great!

（注） accident 事故   get lost 道に迷う   equipment 装備

（ 1 ）	ア became	イ broke	ウ happened	エ returned
（ 2 ）	ア at last	イ because of	ウ next to	エ of course
（ 3 ）	ア remembered	イ disappeared	ウ removed	エ practiced
（ 4 ）	ア himself	イ myself	ウ themselves	エ yourself
（ 5 ）	ア collected	イ shared	ウ needed	エ worked

4　次の1～5の会話文の（　　　）内の語句を並べ替え，それぞれの文を完成しなさい。解答欄には，（　　　）内において3番目と5番目にくるものの記号を書きなさい。

1　A: Do you have any brothers or sisters?

　　B: I have a sister. She is still a baby.

　　A: Do you (ア of　イ like　ウ care　エ sister　オ taking　カ your)?

　　B: Of course. She is very cute.

2　A: Mary is coming back from America today. Shall we go to the airport to see her?

　　B: Do you know (ア plane　イ arrive　ウ her　エ time　オ will　カ what)?

　　A: Yes. At 10:30.

3　A: Why do you know so many things about Taro?

　　B: Because we (ア each　イ have　ウ we　エ known　オ other　カ since) were children.

4　A: Excuse me. Can (ア me　イ tell　ウ shortest　エ the　オ you　カ way) to the station?

　　B: Sure. Go straight along this street to the bank. Turn right at the corner.

5　A: What are you doing?

　　B: I am practicing my English speech. The (ア Ms. Smith　イ have　ウ make　エ students　オ teaches　カ to) speeches in class.

5 次の文章をよく読んで，後の問題に答えなさい。

Takashi is a junior high student. He has a brother and a sister. His brother Hiroshi is ten years old and his sister Tomoko is five years old.

Julie is also a junior high student who lives next to Takashi's house. She lives with her parents and her sister. Julie's sister Ann is a high school student.

One day, Takashi and his family went to *karaoke*. They checked in at eleven in the morning. First, Takashi's parents sang a song together. Then Takashi sang a song by his favorite group, ABC 47. Next, his brother and sister sang a children's song together. After that, Takashi's father sang two songs and his mother sang her favorite song.

At noon, they felt hungry. So they ordered a large pizza and some drinks. Thirty minutes later, Julie's family came to the same place and checked in. Then they found Takashi's family and joined them. Julie's mother likes the songs of ABC 47 but she cannot sing them well. So she asked Takashi to sing one of ABC 47's songs, and he did. Julie's father did not come because he had to work that day. Julie and her mother sang two songs together. Then Julie sang a song with Ann, and another song with Takashi. The song she sang with Takashi was also ABC 47's.

At one twenty, the two families finished singing and went home. Takashi's father paid for all of the *karaoke* charges and food.

(注)　check in　受付をする　　　ABC 47　（架空の歌手グループ名）
　　　order　注文する　　　　　paid for ～　～の料金を支払った　　　charge　料金

料金表（消費税込）				
カラオケ	時　間	1 時間まで	2 時間まで	3 時間まで
	大　　　人	￥ 500	￥ 800	￥ 1,000
	中学・高校生	￥ 300	￥ 600	￥ 800
	小学生以下	無　料		
食べ物	ピ　ザ		焼きそば	
	大 ￥ 1,000 ／ 小 ￥ 600		大 ￥ 500 ／ 小 ￥ 400	
飲み物	無　料			

[問題]　本文およびその下の料金表をもとに，次の１～５の英文の（　　　　）に入る適切なものを
　　　　ア～エの中からそれぞれ一つずつ選び，記号で答えなさい。

1　（　　　　）songs were sung in the morning.
　　ア　Six　　　　　　　イ　Seven　　　　　ウ　Eight　　　　　エ　Nine

2　Julie sang（　　　　）songs that day.
　　ア　two　　　　　　　イ　three　　　　　ウ　four　　　　　エ　five

3　Takashi sang（　　　　）songs by ABC 47 that day.
　　ア　two　　　　　　　イ　three　　　　　ウ　four　　　　　エ　five

4　（　　　　）people went to *karaoke* that day.
　　ア　Six　　　　　　　イ　Seven　　　　　ウ　Eight　　　　　エ　Nine

5　Takashi's father paid（　　　　）for all of the *karaoke* charges and food.
　　ア　3,600 yen　　　　イ　4,900 yen　　　ウ　5,200 yen　　　エ　5,800 yen

（メモ，計算用余白）

6 次の文章およびその下のグラフをよく読んで，後の問いに答えなさい。

　　Different animals have different hours of sleeping. Some animals sleep for only a few hours each day. Other animals sleep longer, and some sleep for half the day or more.

　　There are many reasons for these differences. Perhaps the most important reason is the animal's size. Usually, 【　A　】. For example, small animals like bats sleep for twenty hours each day. However, big animals such as elephants, giraffes and horses all sleep for about four hours each day.

　　There is another reason. Animals that hunt, like lions and tigers, sleep longer because they don't have to be afraid of other animals. Animals that are hunted, such as deer, sleep for only a few hours each day. If they sleep for many hours, some other animals may catch them. ア

　　The age of the animal is another reason. Like humans, animals have different hours of sleeping at different ages. For example, young animals usually need to sleep more than older animals. イ

　　When animals are caught and put in a zoo, the number of hours they sleep will also change. Animals often get more sleep when they are in a zoo than they do in the wild. Food is given to them, and they are safe from animals that hunt them. ウ

　　However, animals that live in the wild have to hunt or gather their food for many hours each day. Some animals have to travel a long way 【　B　】. Many also have to be careful when dangerous animals are near them. So, they may sleep for fewer hours in their ⬚ environment.

　　For example, the slow-moving sloth in a zoo sleeps for about 16 hours each day. A team of scientists went to a rainforest to study sloths. They discovered that sloths slept for about 10 hours each day in their ⬚ environment.

(注)　each day　１日あたり　　　half the day　半日　　　bat　コウモリ
　　　giraffe　キリン　　　　　　hunt　狩りをする　　　　deer　シカ
　　　the wild　野生の状態　　　sloth　ナマケモノ　　　rainforest　熱帯雨林

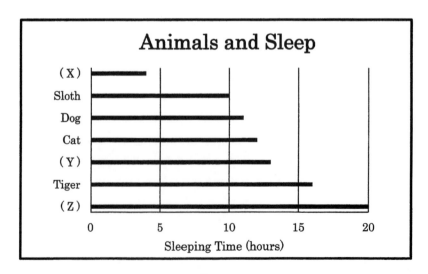

問1　本文中の　【　A　】と【　B　】に入れるのに適切なものを次のア～ウの中から一つずつ選び，記号で答えなさい。

【　A　】

ア　smaller animals sleep as long as larger animals

イ　smaller animals sleep longer than larger animals

ウ　larger animals sleep longer than smaller animals

【　B　】

ア　to go abroad

イ　to live in a zoo

ウ　to find their food

問2　次の英文を入れるのに適切な位置を本文中の　ア　～　ウ　の中から一つ選び，記号で答えなさい。

　　So they can relax and sleep longer.

問3　グラフの　(X), (Y), (Z) は，それぞれある動物を表しています。その正しい組み合わせを，次のア～エの中から一つ選び，記号で答えなさい。

ア　(X) Bat　　　　　(Y) Lion　　　　(Z) Elephant

イ　(X) Elephant　　(Y) Lion　　　　(Z) Bat

ウ　(X) Elephant　　(Y) Bat　　　　 (Z) Lion

エ　(X) Lion　　　　 (Y) Elephant　　(Z) Bat

問4　本文の内容と合うように，次の1と2の下線部に入る適切なものをそれぞれ下のア～ウの中から一つずつ選び，記号で答えなさい。

　　1　Older animals usually sleep _____.

　　ア　for more hours than baby animals

　　イ　for fewer hours than baby animals

　　ウ　for the same number of hours as baby animals

　　2　Animals that are hunted usually sleep for fewer hours than animals that hunt _____.

　　ア　because they are afraid of animals that hunt

　　イ　because they have to catch other animals

　　ウ　because they are usually very small

問5　本文とグラフの内容に合うものを次のア～ウの中から一つ選び，記号で答えなさい。

　　ア　Horses sleep for more hours than dogs because their size is larger.

　　イ　Cats sleep for fewer hours than horses because cats are smaller.

　　ウ　Both tigers and dogs sleep longer than horses.

問6　本文中の2か所の _____ に共通して入る適切な1語を英語で書きなさい。なお，その語はnで始まり，解答欄のマス目の数と同じ文字数の語です。解答欄に書かれた1文字目に続けて正しくつづりなさい。

1　次の(1)〜(5)の各組の英文において，**ア**と**イ**の文中の（　　　）に共通する適切な1語を入れなさ
い。なお，その語は解答欄のマス目の数と同じ文字数の語です。解答欄に書かれた1文字目に続
けて正しくつづりなさい。

(1)　**ア**　That building is very old. It's almost one (t　　) years old.

　　　イ　If you add five hundred to five hundred, you get one (t　　).

(2)　**ア**　When you (t　　) something with your hand, you put your hand on it and feel it.

　　　イ　Don't (t　　) the wall because I just finished painting it.

(3)　**ア**　I have to go to school every (S　　) this year.

　　　イ　Sunday comes after (S　　).

(4)　**ア**　To (u　　) is to know what something means or why something happens.

　　　イ　When you are young, you should learn a foreign language to (u　　) other
　　　cultures.

(5)　**ア**　Would you like to leave a (m　　)?

　　　イ　A (m　　) is a written or spoken piece of information that you send to someone.

2 次の１～５の会話文の（　　　）に入る適切なものを，それぞれ下の**ア**～**エ**の中から一つずつ選び，記号で答えなさい。

1　A: Hello, this is John. Can I speak to Mary, please?
　　B: There is no one named Mary here. （　　）
　　A: Oh, I'm sorry.
　　　ア　She will be busy.　　　　　　　**イ**　You are welcome.
　　　ウ　You have the wrong number.　　　**エ**　She has just come here.

2　A: Would you like to have some more pie?
　　B: No, thank you. （　　）
　　A: Then, how about another cup of coffee?
　　　ア　I've had enough.　　　　　　　**イ**　I can't drink any more.
　　　ウ　I want to eat some more pie.　　**エ**　I didn't have any pie.

3　A: I guess you don't live near here.
　　B: Why do you think so?
　　A: （　　）
　　B: Oh, you did? Yes, you are right. I live far from here.
　　　ア　Because you and I were not at the meeting.
　　　イ　You don't think I am wrong.
　　　ウ　You usually take a bus to get to school.
　　　エ　I saw you on the train this morning.

4　A: When are we going to eat?
　　B: （　　）
　　A: What kind of food do they serve?
　　B: They have good hamburgers.
　　A: That's fine. Let's go there together.
　　　ア　I want some Japanese food.　　　**イ**　Well, the restaurant will open at 5:00.
　　　ウ　We've already closed for tonight.　**エ**　I have some hamburgers.

5　A: Do you like this movie?
　　B: Yes, I do.
　　A: （　　）
　　B: Three times.
　　　ア　How many times have you seen it?　**イ**　When did you see it?
　　　ウ　Do you have the time?　　　　　**エ**　What time will you see it?

3 次の文章中の（ 1 ）～（ 5 ）に入る適切なものを，それぞれ下の**ア**～**エ**の中から一つずつ選び，記号で答えなさい。

Wilma Rudolph was a star in track and field in the 1960 Olympics. She won three gold medals. People （ 1 ） her "the fastest woman in the world."

However, when she was a young child, Wilma Rudolph could not play sports. She was weak and often sick, and then, she got polio. She （ 2 ） the use of her left leg, and the doctors said she would never walk again.

Wilma's family was very large and was very poor, but they did as （ 3 ） as they could to help her. Wilma and her mother often traveled more than 100 km to go to the doctor for her leg. Her brothers and sisters gave her leg a massage every day. They also helped her when she did special exercises for her leg. By the time Wilma was nine years old, she （ 4 ） walk again. Soon, she started playing basketball and running. In high school, she was a track star, and then she went to the Olympics.

She continued running, and later, when she was twenty-two years old, she became a teacher and track coach. Her story gave many people the courage （ 5 ） hard even in difficult situations.

(注) track and field　陸上競技　　　　　gold medal　金メダル
polio　ポリオ(病気の名前)　　　　massage　マッサージ
exercise　運動　　　　　　　　　by the time ～　～のころまでには
courage　勇気　　　　　　　　　situation　状況

（ 1 ）　**ア**　called　　　**イ**　said　　　**ウ**　spoke　　　**エ**　told
（ 2 ）　**ア**　got　　　　**イ**　had　　　**ウ**　lost　　　**エ**　made
（ 3 ）　**ア**　fast　　　**イ**　many　　　**ウ**　much　　　**エ**　soon
（ 4 ）　**ア**　can　　　**イ**　cannot　　**ウ**　did not　　**エ**　was able to
（ 5 ）　**ア**　to work　　**イ**　work　　　**ウ**　worked　　**エ**　working

4 次の1～5の会話文の（　　　）内の語句を並べ替え，それぞれの文を完成しなさい。解答欄には，（　　　）内において3番目と5番目にくるものの記号を書きなさい。

1 A: Which country shall we visit this summer?

　　B: I think Japan is good because it (ア beautiful イ is ウ most エ of オ one カ the) countries in the world.

2 A: I heard a new stadium will be built in our city. Did you hear that, too?

　　B: Yes, it's (ア am イ I ウ in エ reading オ the newspaper カ written) now.

3 A: I (ア a lot イ is ウ listening エ music オ think カ to) of fun.

　　B: What kind of music do you like?

　　A: I like pop music.

4 A: I want to buy a new computer. Could (ア buy イ me ウ tell エ to オ where カ you) a good one?

　　B: Sure. Let's go shopping together.

5 A: Did Japan win the game last night?

　　B: I don't know because I (ア busy イ the game ウ to エ too オ was カ watch) on TV last night.

5　次の文章をよく読んで，後の問題に答えなさい。

　　One day, Mayumi and her mother went shopping in a department store. Mayumi wanted to buy some shoes. She found two pairs of shoes that she liked at a shoe shop. One pair was 2,000 yen, and the other pair was 4,000 yen. But she found out that the shop was going to have a "Time Sale" — from one thirty to two o'clock in the afternoon. During the "Time Sale," every pair of shoes in the shop would be half price.

　　Because it was just noon, Mayumi and her mother went down to the food floor to buy some food. Her mother was going to cook curry for dinner that day, so she had to buy potatoes, carrots and meat. In the vegetable shop, potatoes and carrots were sold in 1 kg plastic bags. There were five potatoes in a bag and each bag was sold for 300 yen. Each potato was almost the same size. A bag of four carrots was 360 yen. Her mother bought one bag of potatoes and one bag of carrots. She also had to buy meat, so they went to the meat shop. In the meat shop, 100 g of beef was sold for 200 yen. Her mother bought 200 g of beef and 300 g of pork. She paid 700 yen for the meat.

　　After leaving the food floor, they went back to the shoe shop. They entered the shop just when the "Time Sale" started. Mayumi bought both pairs of shoes she found before.

　（注）　price　値段　　curry　カレー　　beef　牛肉　　pork　豚肉　　paid　支払った

［問題］　本文の内容から考えて，次の1～5の英文の（　　　）に入る適切なものをア～エの中か
　　　　らそれぞれ一つずつ選び，記号で答えなさい。

1　One potato is about （　　　）.
　　ア　60 g　　　　　　イ　100 g　　　　　ウ　200 g　　　　　エ　250 g

2　Mayumi's mother paid （　　　） for vegetables.
　　ア　300 yen　　　　イ　360 yen　　　　ウ　660 yen　　　　エ　700 yen

3　100 g of pork was （　　　）.
　　ア　100 yen　　　　イ　200 yen　　　　ウ　500 yen　　　　エ　700 yen

4　Mayumi paid （　　　） at the shoe shop.
　　ア　3,000 yen　　　イ　4,000 yen　　　ウ　5,000 yen　　　エ　6,000 yen

5　They spent about （　　　） after leaving the shoe shop until they returned there.
　　ア　60 minutes　　　イ　90 minutes　　　ウ　120 minutes　　　エ　240 minutes

6　次の古代マヤ(The Maya)文明についての文章をよく読んで，後の問いに答えなさい。

　　　A long time ago, a group of people lived in the jungles of Mexico and Central America. They were called the Maya people.　Their kings built temples and pyramids, and 【　A　】. They have learned about the history and everyday life of the Maya people by using information which was found in the jungles.　They have found many interesting things about the Maya culture.

　　　The Maya people had a wonderful counting system.　At the time, most of the people in the world 【　B　】.　However, the Maya people were using a round shape like a ring as a symbol to show the number.　Their counting system had only three symbols: a dot for one, a bar for five, and the round shape for zero.　For the Maya people, some numbers were very important.　For example, 20 was special because it was equal to the number of fingers and toes that they could use for counting.　The number 52 was also a special number for the Maya people.

　　　The Maya people also made calendars.　We now use a ［　①　］.　But the Maya people didn't use the ［　②　］ as ours.　They used several ［　③　］ at the same time.

　　　There were 13 months in the calendar called *Tzolkin*.　Each month had 20 days.　This calendar was used by farmers.　*Haab*, another calendar, had 365 days.　The calendar was based on the movement of the earth around the sun.　It had 18 months and five days.　The Maya people thought these last five days were bad luck.　The Maya people used these two calendars at the same time.

　　　The Maya also had a third calendar.　It was called *the Long Count Calendar*. *The Long Count Calendar* started on August 11, 3114 B.C. because they believed that the world was made on this day.　December 21, 2012 was the (　　　　) of this calendar, and some people thought that the world would (　　　　) on that day.

(注)　the jungles of Mexico and Central America　メキシコ・中米地域のジャングル
　　　pyramid　ピラミッド　　　　　　　counting system　数の数え方
　　　shape　形　　　　　　　　　　　　ring　輪
　　　dot　点　　　　　　　　　　　　　bar　棒
　　　equal to ～　～に等しい　　　　　fingers and toes　手と足の指
　　　several　いくつかの　　　　　　　based on ～　～にもとづいて
　　　movement　動き　　　　　　　　　B.C.　紀元前

問1　本文中の【　A　】と【　B　】に入れるのに適切なものを次の**ア**～**ウ**の中から一つずつ選び，記号で答えなさい。

【　A　】

ア　they are now very important for scientists

イ　they are studying very hard to build temples and pyramids

ウ　they can find some information about their culture

【　B　】

ア　learned how to count from the Maya people

イ　used the same symbols that the Maya people used

ウ　didn't have any knowledge about the number zero

問2　下の四角の中に描かれたものは，ある数をマヤ文明で使われていた記号で表したものです。これを私たちが現在使用している数字で表すとどうなるか，その数字を**ア**～**エ**の中から一つ選び，記号で答えなさい。

ア　7

イ　19

ウ　23

エ　34

問3　本文中の　①　～　③　に入れる語句として正しい組み合わせを，次の**ア**～**ウ**の中から一つ選び，記号で答えなさい。

ア　①　same calendar　　②　twelve-month calendar　　③　different calendars

イ　①　different calendar　　②　twelve-month calendar　　③　same calendars

ウ　①　twelve-month calendar　　②　same calendar　　③　different calendars

問4　本文の内容と合うように，次の1と2の下線部に入る適切なものをそれぞれ下の**ア**～**ウ**の中から一つずつ選び，記号で答えなさい。

1　The Maya people _____.

ア　could count only from zero to twenty

イ　used a bar for the number one

ウ　thought 20 and 52 were special numbers

2　The Maya people _____.

ア　made two different calendars to know the movement of the fields

イ　used a calendar which had almost the same number of the days as ours

ウ　thought the last five days of the *Haab* calendar were good

— 7 —

問 5　本文の内容と合うものを次の**ア**～**ウ**の中から一つ選び，記号で答えなさい。

　　ア　The number of days in *Tzolkin* and *Haab* calendars were the same.

　　イ　One of the Maya calendars had 265 days in a Maya year.

　　ウ　There were more than two calendars used by the Maya people.

問 6　本文中の 2 か所の（　　　）に共通して入る適切な 1 語を英語で書きなさい。
　　　ただし，それは e で始まり，本文中に使われていない語とします。

1　次の 1 ～ 5 の会話文の（　　　）の中に適切な 1 語を入れなさい。なお，その語は（　　　）の中に書いてある文字で始まります。解答は与えられた文字も含めて正しくつづりなさい。

1　A: The first month of the year is January. Then, what is the (n　　　) month?
　　B: It's September.

2　A: Most people in Japan speak Japanese.
　　B: Do they learn English as a (f　　　) language at school?
　　A: Yes, they do. They have to learn it for many years.

3　A: Ken, your house is next to ABC High School, but you came to this school. Why?
　　B: That's a good (q　　　), Mary. Because I want to become an engineer.

4　A: It's very hot today. Would you like (s　　　) to drink?
　　B: Yes, please. I want cold water.

5　A: Please (i　　　) yourself.
　　B: My name is John Smith. I'm from Canada.

2 次の1～5の会話文の( )に入る適切なものを，それぞれ下のア～エの中から一つずつ選び，記号で答えなさい。

1 A: I built a new house and moved into it last week.

  B: Really? ( )

  A: It's bigger than my old one and I have my own room.

  ア How can you help me? イ How about this?

  ウ What's it like? エ What's the matter?

2 A: Hello?

  B: Hi, Ms. Green. Is Mary there, please?

  A: I'm sorry she's not here right now. ( )

  B: Yes, please. There's a party at my home on Wednesday.

  ア Will it be all right with you? イ Shall I take a message?

  ウ Could you ask her to call me later? エ Will you call me back later?

3 A: Let's start today's lesson. Tom, ( )

  B: We were on page 125.

  ア where are you? イ which class were you in?

  ウ how have you been? エ where were we last time?

4 A: How about going to a movie with me this weekend?

  B: ( ) I'm free on Saturday.

  A: That's great.

  ア Why not? イ No, I don't.

  ウ Of course not. エ What was that?

5 A: My aunt lives in China.

  B: Oh, I didn't know that. Which part of China does she live in?

  A: ( )

  ア I think she lives in the east.

  イ I think she has lived there for many years.

  ウ I think she does.

  エ I don't think so.

— 2 —

3　次の文章中の（　1　）～（　5　）に入る適切な語句を，それぞれ下の**ア**～**エ**の中から一つずつ選び，記号で答えなさい。

In 1975, Ms. Tabei Junko stood on the top of the world.　She has always climbed mountains.　When she was ten, she climbed Mt. Nasu with her classmates and teachers. Then she （　1　） that she loved climbing.

Over the years she climbed many mountains with her friends and family.　In 1971, she （　2　） a group which was planning a big climb.　Every night she prepared for the climb by jogging.

Early in 1975, Ms. Tabei and her group went to Nepal.　While they were climbing, they had a lot of problems.　They were out of breath from the lack of oxygen.　It was −30 ℃ at night.　Above 7,000 meters, they could climb only 300 meters in a day.

Sometimes she wanted to （　3　）.　But she kept climbing and （　4　） she stood on the top of Mt. Chomolungma, the highest mountain in the world.

Why does Ms. Tabei love climbing?

The best answer is in her own words.　"You can stand on the top of any mountain if you walk step by step.　You don't have to walk fast.　You （　5　） have to keep walking."

(注)　climb　（～に）登る，登山　　　over the years　長年にわたって　　Nepal　ネパール
out of breath　息を切らして　　lack of oxygen　酸素不足
Chomolungma　チョモランマ（エベレストのチベット名）

（　1　）　**ア**　came back　　**イ**　looked at　　**ウ**　talked to　　**エ**　found out
（　2　）　**ア**　joined　　　**イ**　looked　　　**ウ**　traveled　　**エ**　happened
（　3　）　**ア**　take out　　**イ**　give up　　　**ウ**　think of　　**エ**　worry about
（　4　）　**ア**　right now　　**イ**　some day　　**ウ**　at last　　　**エ**　thanks to
（　5　）　**ア**　once　　　　**イ**　only　　　　**ウ**　most　　　　**エ**　quickly

4 次の1〜5の英文の(　　)内の語句を並べ替え，それぞれの文を完成しなさい。答えの欄には，(　　)内において3番目と5番目にくるものの記号を書きなさい。

1　A: Happy birthday! Do you remember our plan for tonight?

　B: Yes, of course.　I'm (ア going　to　イ with　ウ to　エ looking　オ the　concert　カ forward) you.

2　A: Is this (ア that　イ looking　ウ you　エ for　オ were　カ the key)?

　B: That's it! Thank you. Where did you find it?

3　A: You have many good friends. He looks like your best friend.

　B: Yes.　He and I (ア since　イ other　ウ known　エ we　オ have　カ each) were young.

4　A: Do you know the man on this poster?

　B: Yes, he (ア a tennis player　イ loved　ウ many　エ is　オ young　カ by) girls in Japan.

5　A: Have you bought a Christmas present for Mary?

　B: Well, I found a good thing, but it was (ア I　イ that　ウ buy　エ so　オ couldn't　カ expensive) it.

5　次の文章をよく読んで，後の問題に答えなさい。

Have you ever heard of the triathlon?　If you take part in a triathlon race, you have to swim, ride a bike, and run with no breaks.

One day, Mr. Yamada took part in a triathlon race.　The distances for the men's course were 1.5 km for the swimming part, 40 km for the cycling part, and the total distance of the race was 51.5 km.　The race started at nine o'clock in the morning.

In this race, Mr. Yamada took thirty minutes for the swimming part.　Then he took one hour and twenty minutes for the cycling part.　In the last part, he ran for fifty minutes to finish the race.

Mr. Tanaka also took part in the race.　He finished the swimming part faster than Mr. Yamada, and the difference was five minutes.　But he took longer than Mr. Yamada in the cycling part, and the difference for the cycling part was ten minutes.　At last, they finished the race at the same time.

The triathlon race had another course for women.　The distance of the women's swimming part was 1 km, and the distances of the cycling part and the running part were half of the distances of the men's course.

Mrs. Yamada took part in the women's race.　She could swim, ride a bike, and run as fast as Mr. Yamada.　The women's race started at the same time as the men's race started.

(注)　triathlon　トライアスロン　　　take part in ～　～に参加する　　　distance　距離
　　　cycling　自転車で走ること　　　total　合計の

[問題]　本文の内容から考えて，次の1～5の英文の（　　）に入る適切なものをア～エの中か
　　　らそれぞれ一つずつ選び，記号で答えなさい。

1　Mr. Yamada finished his race at (　　) a.m.

　ア　11:20　　　　　イ　11:30　　　　　ウ　11:32　　　　　エ　11:40

2　Mr. Tanaka finished his cycling part at (　　) a.m.

　ア　10:40　　　　　イ　10:50　　　　　ウ　10:55　　　　　エ　11:05

3　Mr. Tanaka took (　　) minutes for the running part.

　ア　30　　　　　　イ　45　　　　　　ウ　50　　　　　　エ　80

4　The total distance of women's course was (　　) km.

　ア　25.75　　　　　イ　26　　　　　　ウ　51　　　　　　エ　50.75

5　Mrs. Yamada finished her race at (　　) a.m.

　ア　10:25　　　　　イ　10:40　　　　　ウ　11:25　　　　　エ　11:40

— 5 —

6 　以下は，あるテレビ番組における総合司会者の Lisa と３人のレポーターとの会話です。よく読んで，後の問いに答えなさい。

Lisa: People have very different ideas for their dream home, or their perfect house. Some people want to live in a simple house in a special place, 【 A 】 Is your dream home a large house, a simple one, or a special one? Let's look at some dream homes in tonight's 'World Report'.

John: Good evening. This is John Clark, near the Arabian Sea. Look at this tall building. I am now standing in front of the most expensive house in the world. One of the richest businesspersons from Japan, Yaguchi Kazuko, owns this dream house. She has many hotels and department stores all over the world. The house has 27 floors, so it has enough rooms for everything her family needs and wants. It was built last year. Ms. Yaguchi has a lot of cars, so the first six floors from the ground are for cars. The next floor of the house has a movie room with seats for 50 people. Then the next two floors of the house are for a swimming pool and a gym. There are some floors for people who are invited to stay. They can relax in large, beautiful gardens on the 14th and 15th floors. The four floors at the top of the building are only for the Yaguchi family. From there, they have a great view of the Arabian Sea.

Lisa: Wow, it's a great view, isn't it? But I think there are too many rooms. Who cleans all the rooms?

John: That's a good point, Lisa. Well, Ms. Yaguchi doesn't clean her house at all because 【 B 】

Lisa: Wow! That's great! I hope to be rich like her in the future. Thanks, John. The next report is from Paul Brown.

Paul: Hi, this is Paul Brown, how are you doing tonight? Carl Masterson is known as a great American writer who wrote many stories about American nature. He was born in 1824. Twenty-eight years later, he built this perfect house and started to live in it. It was the year after he wrote his first book. Then he lived here for a long time until he died at the age of 48. As you can see, it is a very small house. In the house, there were three chairs, a bed, a table, and a small desk. It was a simple house but the location of his house was very important to Masterson. He built his house in the forest and there is a beautiful lake in front of the house. Look at this view!

Lisa: Oh, the lake is so beautiful! I love it. Masterson's house is really small but I think 【 C 】 Thanks, Paul. The next report is from Africa. Please begin, David.

David: Good evening. This is a report from the Democratic Republic of the Congo. Claude Milongo is a 29-year-old famous soccer player. He is now playing and living in France

— 6 —

and he built his dream home here two years ago. Claude was born on January 1, 1984 and grew up in the Congo, but he and his family moved to France when he was eight. He wanted to be a doctor, but he became a famous soccer player. Claude's dream home is in the Congo and it has beds for 200 people. 【 D 】he built it for the people in his home country instead. Many doctors and nurses are working there. Yes, Claude's dream home is a [   ]!

Lisa: Wow, I like his story. Claude built a great dream home! How wonderful! That's why so many people in the world love him very much. OK, now everyone, what is your dream home? Large, simple, or special? This is the end of tonight's 'World Report'. Good night.

(注) the Arabian Sea アラビア海   businessperson 実業家   own ～ ～を所有する
      floor 階   location 所在地
      the Democratic Republic of the Congo コンゴ民主共和国   instead その代わりに
      That's why ～ そういうわけで～

問１ 本文中の【 A 】～【 D 】に入る適切なものを，それぞれ下のア～ウの中から一つずつ
    選び，記号で答えなさい。

【 A 】

ア because no one hopes to build a small and simple house to live in.

イ and they build a large and tall house with beautiful gardens in it.

ウ but others want to live in a large house with many things for their lives.

【 B 】

ア she has many cleaning robots and they clean all the rooms.

イ half of the floors of the house are only for cars and she doesn't have to clean all the rooms.

ウ she has lived in the house for five years and she has many helpers.

【 C 】

ア he loved the house because he was born there.

イ he needed a quiet and beautiful place for writing.

ウ he liked it and lived there alone for 48 years.

【 D 】

ア Claude didn't build his dream home for himself but

イ Claude wanted to become a doctor because

ウ Claude was not loved by most people in France because

— 7 —

問2　本文中の下線部を説明した文として<u>正しくないもの</u>を，次の**ア〜ウ**の中から一つ選び，記号で答えなさい。

　　ア　There are large, beautiful gardens in the building, and the floors for cars are in the lower part of it.

　　イ　The building stands near the Arabian Sea and a great view of the sea can be seen from the higher floors of it.

　　ウ　Four floors are for the family who owns the building and twenty-seven other floors are for the people who are invited.

問3　本文の内容と合うものを次の**ア〜カ**の中から二つ選び，記号で答えなさい。

　　ア　There are many beds in Carl's dream home.

　　イ　Claude and his family left for France in 1992.

　　ウ　Ms. Yaguchi has a gym on the second floor of her house.

　　エ　Carl lived in his dream home for 37 years.

　　オ　Masterson built his dream house in 1852.

　　カ　Masterson wrote his first book when he was 29 years old.

問4　本文中の ☐ に入る適切な1語を英語で書きなさい。ただし，それは<u>hで始まり，本文中に使われていない語</u>とします。

1　次の1〜6の会話文の（　　　）の中に適切な1語を入れなさい。なお，その語は（　　　）の中
に書いてある文字で始まります。解答は与えられた文字も含めて正しくつづりなさい。

1　A: What do you want to be in the (f　　　)?

　　B: I want to be an astronaut.

2　A: What are you looking at?

　　B: I'm looking at old pictures (t　　　) twenty years ago.

3　A: What (l　　　) is spoken in your country?

　　B: Most people use English.

4　A: Which mountain is the (h　　　) in Japan?

　　B: Mt. Fuji is. It's 3,776 meters to the top.

5　A: What month comes just before September?

　　B: (A　　　) does.

6　A: How long will the Olympic Games (l　　　)?

　　B: For about two weeks.

2　次の１～６の会話文の（　　　）に入る適切なものを，それぞれ下のア～エの中から一つずつ選び，記号で答えなさい。

1　A: I'm so tired tonight.
　　B: OK, Dad. （　　　　　）
　　A: Thanks, but you don't have to.
　　　ア　You look bad.　　　　　　　イ　I know you are.
　　　ウ　You should go to bed.　　　　エ　I will cook for you.

2　A: I lost my bag on the train. There were many important things in it.
　　B: （　　　　　）
　　A: I don't remember its name, but it was from Fifth Street to Central Station.
　　　ア　Excuse me, what did you say?　　イ　Which line did you take?
　　　ウ　What was in your bag?　　　　エ　May I have your name, please?

3　A: （　　　　　）
　　B: Of course, you can.
　　A: Wow! I wanted to buy this myself. Was it expensive?
　　B: No, it wasn't.
　　　ア　I don't think you made this.　　イ　Can you buy it for me?
　　　ウ　May I open it?　　　　エ　I am going to buy it.

4　A: I would like two tickets to Seoul.
　　B: （　　　　　）
　　A: Around seven this evening.
　　　ア　What time would you like to leave?
　　　イ　When did you go there?
　　　ウ　How many days are you going to stay?
　　　エ　How long will it take to go there?

5　A: Would you like to have dinner with me?
　　B: I'd like to, but （　　　　　）
　　A: Oh, that's too bad.
　　　ア　you have been there once before.　　イ　I can drive by myself.
　　　ウ　I have to work late tonight.　　　　エ　you never wanted to talk about that.

6　A: Do you have a bike that I can use? I need to go to the hospital by noon.
　　B: （　　　　　）
　　A: Oh, OK. Don't worry about it. Thanks.
　　　ア　Let's see... I went there yesterday.　　イ　Sorry, Ken. I'm going to use it later.
　　　ウ　Yes, you can get home soon.　　　　エ　I don't think that is my favorite.

— 2 —

3 次の文章中の（ 1 ）～（ 6 ）に入る適切な語を，それぞれ下のア～エの中から一つずつ選び，記号で答えなさい。

The earth is one of the eight planets （ 1 ） around the sun. It is the only planet that has plants and animals. There are about 300,000 different kinds of plants on the earth. More than one million kinds of animals live here.

The earth looks blue and beautiful when it is （ 2 ） from space. But is it really a good and beautiful place to live today? Many plants and animals are dying out. The air, the seas, and the rivers are getting dirty.

Plants have been on the earth for many years. Some animals eat plants. （ 3 ） animals eat animals that eat plants.

In the （ 4 ） 200 years, many kinds of animals have （ 5 ） out. People have killed animals （ 6 ） their meat and fur. People have also destroyed animals' homes. If animals can't find a place to live, they die out.

(注) die out 絶滅する　　get dirty よごれる　　fur 毛皮　　destroy 破壊する

（ 1 ）	ア	move	イ	moves	ウ	moved	エ	moving
（ 2 ）	ア	sees	イ	saw	ウ	seen	エ	seeing
（ 3 ）	ア	All	イ	Another	ウ	Either	エ	Other
（ 4 ）	ア	early	イ	last	ウ	first	エ	end
（ 5 ）	ア	die	イ	dies	ウ	died	エ	dying
（ 6 ）	ア	for	イ	in	ウ	on	エ	with

4 次の 1 ～ 6 の英文の（　　　　）内の語句を並べ替え，それぞれの文を完成しなさい。答えの欄には，（　　　　）内において 2 番目と 4 番目にくるものの記号を書きなさい。

1　A: How（ア sister　イ your　ウ long　エ the piano　オ does　カ practice）every day?
　　B: For about two hours.

2　A: How many brothers and sisters do you have?
　　B: I have（ア with　イ younger　ウ lives　エ a　オ brother　カ who）my parents.

3　A: It's very hot today, isn't it?　I'm very thirsty.
　　B: Me, too.　Why（ア buy　イ cold　ウ something　エ to　オ don't　カ we）drink?

4　A: Mom often tells us to clean our room.　It's too much.
　　B: Yes, I（ア want　イ say　ウ her　エ that　オ to　カ don't）so often.

5　A: When I feel sad, I always listen to this song.
　　B: Yes, I believe music（ア power　イ make　ウ the　エ us　オ has　カ to）happy.

6　A: Please（ア me　イ use　ウ teach　エ how　オ this　カ to）computer.
　　B: Sure.　What do you want to do with it?

5 次の会話文をよく読んで，後の問いに答えなさい。

Jane: Excuse me, do you speak English?

Mari: Yes, a little. Do you need some help?

Jane: Yes, please. Could you tell me the way to the Plaza Hotel?

Mari: Sure. It's just down this street. Well, I'm going the same way myself. Would you like me to take you there?

Jane: (1) Thank you very much.

Mari: You're welcome.

They start walking.

Mari: Uh... My name is Mari. I'm a college student. (2)

Jane: I'm from Vancouver, Canada. I'm Jane. I just arrived in Japan yesterday.

Mari: Really? My brother goes to a high school in Vancouver.

Jane: Oh, does he? (3)

Mari: No, I haven't, but I hear it is a beautiful place.

Jane: Yes, it's a wonderful city.

Mari: [A]

Jane: I'm going to teach English at Minato College.

Mari: Minato College? My mother teaches English there!

Jane: Really? I would like to meet her.

Mari: I'm sure my mother would like to meet you, too. Can I call you later?

Jane: Sure. Here is my phone number.

After Mari returns home, she talks with Jane on the phone.

Mari: Hello, Jane. This is Mari.

Jane: Oh, hi, Mari.

Mari: I told my mother about you, and she would like you to come for dinner at our house. Do you have any plans for the day after tomorrow?

Jane: Let's see. Today is Thursday, right? I have plans for tomorrow. [B]

Mari: Great. How about meeting at the hotel at five?

Jane: That sounds good. Oh, I can't wait! [C]

Mari: You're welcome. See you then.

Jane: OK. Bye.

(注) Vancouver バンクーバー(カナダの都市)

問1　本文中の（　1　）～（　3　）に入る適切な文を次のア～オの中から一つずつ選び，記号で答えなさい。

 ア　May I ask where you are from?

 イ　How have you been?

 ウ　Have you ever been there?

 エ　Oh, you're very kind.

 オ　Shall we ask where you are from?

問2　本文中の［　A　］～［　C　］に入る適切な文を次のア～オの中から一つずつ選び，記号で答えなさい。

 ア　I have no plans for Friday.

 イ　I'll be free on Saturday.

 ウ　Thank you for calling.

 エ　Why did you come to Japan?

 オ　Your mother is a very good teacher.

問3　本文の内容と合うように，次の英文中の（　ア　）～（　エ　）に入る適切な語を下の［　　　　］の中から選び，必要があれば適切な形に変えて答えなさい。ただし，それぞれの（　　　　）に入れるのは1語だけとします。

 Mari meets Jane, a woman from Vancouver, Canada, and helps her to （　ア　） her way to the Plaza Hotel.　Mari knows that Vancouver is a beautiful place because her brother is （　イ　） there.　Mari is surprised to know that Jane is going to teach English at the same college as Mari's mother is teaching.　After Mari tells her mother about Jane, they decide to （　ウ　） her to their house, and Mari calls her.　Mari is going to meet Jane at the hotel, and they will have dinner at Mari's house.　Jane is looking forward to （　エ　） Mari and her mother.

 ［　study　　travel　　tell　　invite　　find　　meet　　］

6 次の文章をよく読んで，後の問題に答えなさい。

Takashi and Mizuki are friends. They like playing tennis. Last Sunday, they went to a sports store before going to play tennis. Takashi bought ten balls and three bottles of sports drink. He paid 1,890 yen in total. Mizuki bought three bottles of the same sports drink and six of the same balls as Takashi. She paid 1,290 yen in total.

Takashi and Mizuki began to practice tennis at noon with all the balls they bought on that day. They finished practicing tennis at four fifteen. Then they collected their balls but they couldn't find three of them. They gave up looking for them, and Takashi brought eight balls back home.

Takashi's father likes playing tennis, too. He sometimes buys many tennis balls because he is the manager of his tennis team. He usually buys tennis balls from the Internet shop, Net-Sports. You can buy tennis balls for 120 yen each from Net-Sports, and you need to pay 500 yen for shipping. But if you order more than one hundred, they will send you another twenty balls for free with the balls you ordered, and you don't have to pay for shipping. Last week, Takashi's father ordered tennis balls from Net-Sports, and when they arrived, he received one hundred and fifty balls.

(注) paid　お金を払った　　in total　合計で　　manager　監督　　　pay　お金を払う
shipping　配送（料）　　order...(from〜)　（〜に）...を注文する　　for free　無料で

(問題) 本文の内容から考えて，次の1〜6の英文の（　　　）に入る適切なものをア〜エの中からそれぞれ一つずつ選び，記号で答えなさい。

1　Each tennis ball that Takashi and Mizuki bought was （　　　） yen.

ア　150　　　　　　イ　189　　　　　　ウ　2,400　　　　　エ　3,180

2　Each bottle of sports drink that Takashi and Mizuki bought was （　　　） yen.

ア　129　　　　　　イ　130　　　　　　ウ　189　　　　　　エ　390

3　Takashi and Mizuki practiced tennis for （　　　） minutes.

ア　45　　　　　　イ　240　　　　　　ウ　255　　　　　　エ　290

4　Mizuki brought （　　　） balls back home after the tennis practice.

ア　5　　　　　　　イ　6　　　　　　　ウ　7　　　　　　　エ　8

5　Takashi's father paid （　　　） yen for the tennis balls he ordered last week.

ア　15,600　　　　イ　16,100　　　　ウ　18,000　　　　エ　18,500

6　If you buy eighty tennis balls from Net-Sports, you will have to pay （　　　） yen.

ア　7,200　　　　　イ　7,700　　　　　ウ　9,600　　　　　エ　10,100

7 以下は，あるテレビ番組で行われた討論の一部です。よく読んで，後の問いに答えなさい。

Cathy: Hello. This is Cathy Jackson again, with our talk show. Today we're talking about wild animals as pets. We have invited Dr. Robert Jones, an animal doctor who works at the Park Animal Hospital, and Dr. William Baker, a biologist at Nature College. Let's start with you, Dr. Jones. Some people say that wild animals are too dangerous to keep in the home, 【 A 】 Why?

Dr. Jones: There are a lot of wrong stories about these animals as pets. When people keep wild animals in the right way, they are not dangerous at all. Last week someone brought a ball python to my hospital. It was as cute as a baby cat and really friendly. In the last month, I saw a lion, a tiger, and even a bear. They were not dangerous pets.

Cathy: Thank you, Dr. Jones. Now, Dr. Baker, what do you think?

Dr. Baker: I don't agree. First, many of these animals are injured when they are caught. 【 B 】 Also, they don't always have enough space to run and move around in. 【 C 】 And, if we want to talk about the health problems, I have to tell you that some wild animals carry terrible diseases.

Cathy: Dr. Jones, what can people do for both their wild pets and their families to keep them in good health?

Dr. Jones: Well, there are some important things that people have to do when they keep wild animals as pets. Most of these animals have special needs. Look at this. This shows the "Special Needs of Wild Animals." If people understand their needs and give them the things which they want, people can have a lot of fun with them.

Cathy: You're saying 【 D 】 Thank you, Dr. Jones. And we'll talk about those special needs after we take a break. We'll be back soon!

Special Needs of Wild Animals			
Animal	Food	Other Needs	Special Problems
Ball python	only eats small living animals	needs a warm and quiet place to feel safe	can grow to five feet long
Lion	only eats meat which is not cooked	needs a very large space	keeping a pet lion is legal only in some countries
African clawed frog	will eat small fish, and cat or dog food	needs clean water	may run away

(注) biologist 生物学者　　ball python　ボールパイソン(ニシキヘビの一種)
space 場所　　　　health 健康　　　disease 病気　　　needs 必要条件
African clawed frog　アフリカツメガエル　legal　合法的な

問 1　本文中の【　A　】～【　D　】に入る適切なものを，それぞれ下の**ア〜ウ**の中から一つずつ選び，記号で答えなさい。

【　A　】

ア　but you don't agree.　　イ　but you don't feel safe.　　ウ　but they are not injured.

【　B　】

ア　They will run away from their home country.

イ　It's a really terrible experience for them.

ウ　We have to get injured when we catch animals.

【　C　】

ア　It is not good for us to move around.

イ　But it's easy to keep wild animals in our house.

ウ　It is not really good for their health.

【　D　】

ア　we have to save wild animals because many of them are caught around the world.

イ　you should not think carefully when you want to keep a pet for the first time.

ウ　it's not difficult to have wild animals in the home if people keep the rules.

問 2　本文中の下線部⑴を討論の流れに合うように書き換えたものとして適切なものを，次の**ア〜ウ**の中から一つ選び，記号で答えなさい。

ア　If people take wild animals to an animal hospital,

イ　If people follow the rules for taking care of wild animals,

ウ　If people bring wild animals back to their home country,

問 3　本文中の下線部⑵を説明した文として<u>適切でない</u>ものを，次の**ア〜ウ**の中から一つ選び，記号で答えなさい。

ア　Lions like to eat meat but they don't eat cooked meat at all.

イ　People need clean water when they have African clawed frogs in their homes.

ウ　It's not legal to keep ball pythons and African clawed frogs in our homes.

問 4　次の**ア**と**イ**が説明しているものを本文中から抜き出し，英単語1語で答えなさい。

ア　A large wild cat that has yellow and black lines on its body.

イ　A short time when you stop doing something.

— 9 —

問 5　この討論の題名として適切なものを，次のア〜ウの中から一つ選び，記号で答えなさい。

　　ア　What can we do to keep wild animals safe from disease?

　　イ　Is it legal to keep wild animals as pets?

　　ウ　Should we keep wild animals as pets?

問 6　この討論の内容と合うものを次のア〜ウの中から一つ選び，記号で答えなさい。

　　ア　People are interested in keeping wild animals, but it's difficult because they are expensive.

　　イ　Dr. Baker is against Dr. Jones because some wild animals are dangerous to keep as pets.

　　ウ　Dr. Baker says people should keep wild animals because they are cute.

1　次の 1～6 の会話文の（　　　）の中に適切な 1 語を入れなさい。なお，その語は（　　　）の中に書いてある文字で始まります。解答は与えられた文字も含めて正しくつづりなさい。

1　A: Excuse me, but which of these two rackets is mine?

　　B: This one is mine. You can see my name here. So the other is (y　　　).

2　A: Do you think we can play tennis this afternoon?

　　B: No, I don't think so. It has not (s　　　) raining outside.

3　A: I'm not feeling good.

　　B: That's too bad. Why don't you go to see a (d　　　)?

4　A: When did you come back from Sapporo?

　　B: The day before yesterday. Today is Monday, so it was (S　　　).

5　A: Do you know anything about Australia?

　　B: Yes, of course. It is (f　　　) for koalas.

6　A: You have a nice watch, don't you?

　　B: Thank you. My father (b　　　) it for my birthday present.

2 次の１～５の会話文の（　　　　）に入る適切なものを，それぞれ下のア～エの中から一つずつ選び，記号で答えなさい。

1　A: Have you ever been to Europe?

　　B: Well, I lived in Italy.

　　A: (　　　　　　　　)

　　B: For three years.

　　　ア　When did you live there?　　　　イ　How long did you live there?

　　　ウ　How many times?　　　　　　　　エ　Why did you go there?

2　A: You look tired. What's the matter?

　　B: I didn't sleep at all last night.

　　A: (　　　　　　　　)

　　B: I have some tests at school today.

　　　ア　What time did you sleep?　　　　イ　How long did you sleep?

　　　ウ　Why didn't you sleep?　　　　　　エ　Why did you sleep?

3　A: Janet, I need your help.

　　B: What is it?

　　A: I have to go to Korea next week. Will you take care of my dog?

　　B: (　　　　　　　　) I will not be at home next week.

　　　ア　I'd like to, but I can't.　　　　イ　Where have you been?

　　　ウ　I can take you there.　　　　　　エ　Can you help me?

4　A: Excuse me. Can I take pictures in this museum?

　　B: (　　　　　　　　)

　　A: I'm sorry to hear that.

　　　ア　No, I can't.　　　　　　　　　　イ　Thank you.

　　　ウ　Yes, let's.　　　　　　　　　　　エ　I'm afraid not.

5　A: You play soccer very well, Keisuke. How often do you play it?

　　B: (　　　　　　　　)

　　　ア　Since I was seven.　　　　　　　イ　For a long time.

　　　ウ　Almost every day.　　　　　　　エ　After school tomorrow.

3　次の「空気」に関する文章中の（　1　）～（　5　）に入る適切な語を，それぞれ下のア～エの中から一つずつ選び，記号で答えなさい。

Air is all around you. And it is all around the earth. It is just like the peel which covers an orange. Everything on the earth is （　1　） with air, but you can't see it, or smell it. You usually can't feel it, （　2　）. You can feel it only when it's moving. The air that is moving is called wind.

Air is even in water. That's lucky （　3　） fish. They need air to live just like we need air to live. They use the air that is dissolved in the water. They have gills that help them to do this. We can't breathe the air that is dissolved in water because we don't have gills. So when we （　4　） under water for a long time, we have to take air with us. It is just like the astronauts who take air with them on their backs when they go out of their spaceships.

You usually can't see the air in the water, but sometimes you can. When a glass of water is left in a room for an hour or two, you sometimes find little bubbles on the inside of the glass. They are small bubbles of air that （　5　） out of the water.

(注)　peel　（果物などの）皮　　　dissolved　溶けている　　　gills　（魚の）えら
　　　breathe ～　～を吸い込む　　spaceships　宇宙船　　　　bubbles　あわ

(1) ア cover　　　イ covers　　　ウ covered　　　エ covering
(2) ア other　　　イ another　　　ウ or　　　　　エ either
(3) ア for　　　　イ of　　　　　ウ in　　　　　エ at
(4) ア bring　　　イ take　　　　ウ stay　　　　エ give
(5) ア made　　　イ felt　　　　ウ found　　　　エ came

4 次の1～4の英文の（　　　　）内の語句を並べ替え，それぞれの文を完成しなさい。答えの欄には，（　　　）内において3番目と5番目にくるものの記号を書きなさい。

1 I went to New Zealand during the winter vacation. The trip (ア that　イ wonderful　ウ was　エ want　オ I　カ so) to visit there again.

2 In 2010, a Japanese woman flew in the space shuttle. Her name was Yamazaki Naoko. She (ア space　イ to　ウ became　エ Japanese woman　オ go to　カ the second).

3 Once people believed that animals cannot communicate with each other. But (ア shown　イ scientists　ウ that　エ is　オ have　カ this) not true. They say that all animals can communicate with each other.

4 A: Look at this picture. Do you know him?
　 B: No, I don't. Who is he?
　 A: He is Suzuki Ichiro. He is a (ア player　イ is　ウ all over　エ known　オ who　カ baseball) Japan.

5　次の会話文をよく読んで，後の問いに答えなさい。

Sara and Liz are sisters, and Akiko is their mother's friend. The sisters have just arrived in Japan to study at college. They are now on the way to Akiko's house in her car.

Akiko: Sara, you were only three years old when I saw you last. Liz, you were not born then.

Liz: No, I wasn't.

Sara: It's been a long time.

Akiko: (　　　　1　　　　)

Sara: No, not a thing. But I still have a photo of you, me and mom. I was looking forward to seeing you.

Akiko: Me, too! Is this your first visit to Japan, Liz?

Liz: Yes, I'm really excited about it.

Akiko: What are you going to study at college here?

Liz: Japanese language and culture.

Akiko: I see. (　　　　2　　　　)

Liz: Japanese gardens. They are simple and beautiful. I'd like to see a lot of gardens in Kyoto. I heard that some of the most beautiful gardens are there.

Akiko: That's a good idea. Kyoto is about two and a half hours from Tokyo by high-speed train.

Liz: You mean the *Shinkansen*?

Akiko: (　　　　3　　　　)

Liz: Yes, I read a lot about Japan. (　　　　4　　　　)

Akiko: That's great. If you have any questions, please ask me. What are you going to study, Sara?

Sara: I'm going to study about textiles. I'm very interested in traditional Japanese textiles. During my stay, I want to go to some textile factories and history museums.

Akiko: Sounds interesting. (　　　　5　　　　)

Sara: Thank you. By the way, Akiko, our car hasn't moved much.

Akiko: (　　　　6　　　　) The traffic is terrible today.

Sara: How long will it take from here to your house?

Akiko: Well, it usually takes about twenty minutes, but maybe more than an hour today.

Sara: Oh, no!

　（注）　textiles　織物　　　factories　工場　　　traffic　交通量

問1 本文中の（ 1 ）～（ 6 ）に入る適切な文を次の**ア**～**ク**の中から一つずつ選び，記号で答えなさい。

ア I know some Japanese words.

イ I know. You are right.

ウ I have been to Japan.

エ I hope both of you will have a wonderful time.

オ When did you start studying it?

カ Can you remember anything?

キ Oh, you know that word?

ク What are you interested in the most?

問2 本文の内容と合うように，次の英文中の（ **ア** ）～（ **エ** ）に入る適切な語を下の[ ]の中から選び，必要があれば適切な形に変えて答えなさい。ただし，それぞれの（ ）に入れるのは1語だけとします。

Akiko is （ **ア** ） Sara and Liz to her house by car. Sara is very happy to see Akiko again, because she has not met her for a long time.

Sara and Liz are both going to study in Japan. Sara is going to study about traditional Japanese textiles and she wants to （ **イ** ） some factories and museums. Her sister, Liz, is interested in Japanese gardens. She studied a lot about Japan before （ **ウ** ） to Japan. She also knows some Japanese words such as *Shinkansen*. Sara is （ **エ** ） because she finds that their car hasn't moved much.

[visit   come   look   take   worry]

6 次の文章をよく読んで，後の問題に答えなさい。なお，道はすべて直線であるものとし，自動車の乗降および加減速に要する時間は考慮しないこととします。

Naomi lives with her parents and her brother.

One day, Naomi's father went to the lake and her brother went to the sea in their own cars. They left their house at the same time, 9:00 in the morning. Her father drove his car to the west at a speed of 60 km/h, and her brother went to the east at a speed of 80 km/h.

Naomi wanted to visit her grandfather. So she went together with her brother. She got out of the car at 9:45 in the morning and walked 2 km to the west to his house.

The distances from Naomi's home to her father's and brother's destinations were the same. Her brother arrived at the sea at 11:00 in the morning. Later, her father got to the lake.

Naomi's father and brother started for home from the lake and the sea at the same time. They drove at the same speeds as they did in the morning, but her brother took a break at a hamburger shop. At last, they got home at the same time.

(注) west 西　　　　60 km/h 時速60キロメートル　　　east 東
distance 距離　　destinations 目的地

(問題) 本文の内容から考えて，次の1〜4の英文の（　　　）に入る適切なものをア〜エの中からそれぞれ一つずつ選び，記号で答えなさい。

1 At 9:30 in the morning, the distance between the two cars was (　　　).

ア 22 km　　　イ 50 km　　　ウ 70 km　　　エ 100 km

2 The distance between Naomi's house and her grandfather's was (　　　).

ア 43 km　　　イ 47 km　　　ウ 58 km　　　エ 62 km

3 At 11:00 in the morning, Naomi's father had to drive another (　　　) to the lake.

ア 30 minutes　　　イ 40 minutes　　　ウ 50 minutes　　　エ 60 minutes

4 Naomi's brother stayed at the hamburger shop for (　　　).

ア 20 minutes　　　イ 30 minutes　　　ウ 40 minutes　　　エ 60 minutes

7 次の文章をよく読んで，後の問いに答えなさい。

For most of human history, people did not cook their food. When they found something to eat, they just ate it, and some of them got sick. Thousands of years ago, people learned how to use fire for cooking. But humans have also been interested in 【 A 】 For example, a group of people who lived in Africa about 2,000 years ago baked a kind of bread on rocks that were heated by the sun. This was the beginning of solar cooking.

The first experiments in solar cooking began more than 300 years ago. In those days, glass was becoming easier to get and people began to use it for house windows. Soon, people learned that when sunlight passed through a glass window into a closed room, 【 B 】 About 250 years ago, a scientist, Horace de Saussure, thought about why this happened. In 1767, he did an experiment which measured the temperature changes in closed boxes when they were heated by the sun.

De Saussure used five small glass boxes in his first experiment. He put each one inside of the other. The size of the glass on the top of the largest box was about 25 cm × 25 cm and that of the smallest one was about 5 cm × 5 cm. 　1　 → 　2　 → 　3　 → 　4　 It was 87.5℃. Later he built a better heat box and was able to raise the temperature to 109℃. This heat box was later called a 'hot box' and it was a big step for solar cooking.

Now solar cooking is becoming popular among people in many parts of Africa. ア It makes their lives easier. イ They used to walk a long way to collect wood to cook food. ウ An African woman called Eleanor Shinmeall, for example, cooks with the sun. She steps outside of her home. エ She opens the glass door of the heat box and says, "Ah, it's doing a good job!"

(注)　bread　パン　　　　　　　　　　　　heat　〜を熱する，熱
　　　solar cooking　太陽熱を利用した調理　　experiment　実験
　　　sunlight　太陽光　　　　　　　　　　measure 〜　〜を測る
　　　temperature　温度　　　　　　　　　wood　木

問1　本文中の【　A　】と【　B　】に入る適切なものを，それぞれ下のア〜エの中から一つずつ選び，記号で答えなさい。

【　A　】

ア　how to cook their food with fire in the kitchen.

イ　how to make a fire using the heat from the sun.

ウ　using their hands and fingers when they ate food.

エ　using the heat from the sun to cook their food.

【　B　】

ア　the delicious food was made in the box.

イ　heat energy was changed into light energy.

ウ　the air in the room became warmer.

エ　the heat got out of the clear glass box.

問2　文中の実験を説明する図として適切なものを次のア〜エの中から一つ選び，記号で答えなさい。ただし，それぞれの図は真上から見たようすを示しています。

問 3　本文中の空欄 ┌ 1 ┐ ～ ┌ 4 ┐ には次のア～エの英文が入ります。文脈に合うように正しく並べ替え，記号で答えなさい。

　　ア　The temperature in the smallest box was the highest of all.

　　イ　He used it because he knew something black would catch sunlight better.

　　ウ　After a few hours, he measured the temperatures in the boxes.

　　エ　He put the glass boxes on a black table.

問 4　次の英文を入れるのに適切な位置を本文中の ┌ア┐ ～ ┌エ┐ の中から一つ選び，記号で答えなさい。

　　But now, with the sun and the box, they can cook anything they want to eat.

問 5　本文の内容と合うように，次の 1 と 2 の下線部に入る適切なものをそれぞれ下のア～エの中から一つずつ選び，記号で答えなさい。

　　1　The scientist did an experiment to _____.

　　　ア　measure the temperature changes in the boxes

　　　イ　find the temperature changes in Africa

　　　ウ　bake a kind of bread on rocks

　　　エ　know the temperature of the sun

　　2　Eleanor Shinmeall thinks that the heat box is _____.

　　　ア　popular among people who want to find a good job

　　　イ　used to collect wood to cook food

　　　ウ　useful because she doesn't have to look for wood for cooking

　　　エ　good for measuring the temperature outside of her home

問 6　本文の内容と合うものを次のア～エの中から一つ選び，記号で答えなさい。

　　ア　Thousands of years ago, people started solar cooking with glass boxes.

　　イ　In the heat box, light energy from the sun changes into heat energy.

　　ウ　In the experiment, sunlight didn't pass through the largest glass box.

　　エ　People used to cut trees because they needed wood for solar cooking.

1 次の１～６の会話文の（　　　）の中に最も適当な語を入れなさい。なお，その語は（　　　）の中に書いてある文字で始まります。与えられた文字も含めて正しくつづりなさい。

1 A: Have you ever lived in Hokkaido?

 B: Yes. The weather was (d　　　) from that in Tokyo.

2 A: Did you get a Christmas (p　　　) last year?

 B: Yes. I got a new bike from my parents.

3 A: How did you spend your summer (v　　　)?

 B: I visited Okinawa with my family. We swam a lot.

4 A: Where is the nearest post office?

 B: It's in (f　　　) of the park over there.

5 A: Hello. May I speak to Mr. Sato, please?

 B: I'm afraid you have the (w　　　) number.
 There is no Mr. Sato here.

6 A: I hear there is a lot of snow in the mountains now.

 B: Really? Then, why don't we go (s　　　) this weekend?

2 次の1～5の会話文の(　　　　)に入る最も適当なものを，それぞれ下のア～エの中から一つずつ選び，記号で答えなさい。

1　A: Would you like some coffee?

　　B: (　　　　　　　　)

　　A: Then would you like something else to drink?

　　　ア　Two coffees, please.　　　　イ　Yes. I like it.

　　　ウ　No, thank you.　　　　　　エ　With sugar, please.

2　A: Can I help you?

　　B: (　　　　　　　　)

　　A: Sure. It leaves at 2:45.

　　　ア　Is there a train to Chicago this afternoon?

　　　イ　Where can I take a train to Chicago?

　　　ウ　How long do I have to wait?

　　　エ　Where can I put my bag?

3　A: I'm going to stay here in Japan for two weeks.

　　B: (　　　　　　　　)

　　A: As many temples as I can.

　　　ア　Are there many temples?　　　イ　What do you want to see?

　　　ウ　What can I do for you?　　　エ　Can I see many temples?

4　A: Have you finished cleaning the living room?

　　B: Yes, I have. But I still have to clean the kitchen.

　　A: Do you want me to help you this afternoon?

　　B: (　　　　　　　　)

　　　ア　Yes. I can do it by myself.　　イ　I'm sorry. I can't help you.

　　　ウ　No. I have to wash the car.　　エ　Really?　You are very kind.

5　A: Hello. I'd like to talk with Ms. Jackson.

　　B: She is not at her desk right now.

　　A: (　　　　　　　　)

　　B: Yes, of course. I'll get a pencil.

　　　ア　When can she call me back?　　イ　When will she be back?

　　　ウ　Can I leave my number?　　　エ　Do you know where she is?

3 次のキュリー夫人(Madame Curie)に関する文章中の(1)～(5)に入る最も適当な語を，それぞれ下のア～エの中から一つずつ選び，記号で答えなさい。

Madame Curie is a famous scientist. She lived in Poland and was called Manya when she was young. She was the youngest of five children in her family. She was a very bright girl, and at school she studied with the older girls. At the age of 16, she finished high school with honors.

Even after she left school, she did not (1) studying. For some months she taught children in her town. During this time, Manya decided that she wanted to go to university, but at that time girls could not enter university in Poland. They had to go to (2) country to study. Many people went to Paris to study.

Manya had a sister who also wanted to study at university. But the family was too poor. One day Manya said to her sister, "Bronya, you're twenty and I'm seventeen. So, you should go to Paris to study (3). I'll work here and (4) you some money."

Six years (5) Manya was able to join Bronya in Paris. Manya studied very hard and became a top student at the university in Paris.

(注) Poland ポーランド　bright 頭の良い　with honors 優秀な成績で
　　　university 大学　enter～ ～に入学する　Paris パリ

(1)　ア go　イ keep　ウ enjoy　エ stop
(2)　ア many　イ another　ウ the　エ each
(3)　ア next　イ early　ウ finally　エ first
(4)　ア send　イ show　ウ ask　エ spend
(5)　ア past　イ late　ウ later　エ away

— 3 —

❽⓪

4 次の英文は Jim が古着屋に行った時の話です。下線部(1)〜(4)とほぼ同じ意味になるように、下の英文(1)〜(4)の（　　）内の語句を並べ替え、英文を完成しなさい。答えの欄には、（　　）内において3番目と5番目にくるものの記号を書きなさい。

Jim walked into a store which had a sign outside: "Secondhand Clothes Bought and Sold." He was carrying an old shirt and asked the owner of the store, "このシャツはいくらで買ってくれますか。" The man looked at it and
(1)
said, "Twenty dollars."

"What!" said Jim. "それは50ドルかそれ以上かと思っていました。" "No,"
(2)
said the man, "It is not very nice and should not be more than twenty dollars."

"Are you sure?" asked Jim.

"Very sure," said the man.

"Well," said Jim. 彼はポケットから20ドルを取り出した。 Then he said,
(3)
"Here's twenty dollars. This shirt was in the window of your store with a price of sixty dollars. しかしそれは高すぎると思っていました。 So I wanted to
(4)
know its real price. Thank you for telling me the truth."

Then Jim left the store with the shirt.

(注)　secondhand clothes　古着　　　owner　所有者
　　　price　値段　　　　　　　　　truth　真実

(1) How (ア for　イ me　ウ you　エ will　オ give　カ much) this shirt?

(2) I (ア was　イ more　ウ it　エ or　オ thought　カ fifty dollars).

(3) He (ア twenty dollars　イ his　ウ took　エ of　オ pocket　カ out).

(4) But I (ア too　イ was　ウ believed　エ that　オ much) money.

5 次は客(customer)と店主(manager)の会話文です。よく読んで，後の問いに
答えなさい。

Customer: Good morning. I'd like to speak to the manager.

Manager: I am the manager. How can I help you?

Customer: Well, it's this CD player. (1   )

Manager: Hmm... did you buy it here?

Customer: What? Of course I bought it here yesterday. Look, turn it on and
nothing happens.

Manager: May I see your receipt?

Customer: Receipt? (2   )

Manager: You got a receipt when you bought it.

Customer: Maybe I did, but I don't have it now.

Manager: That's too bad. Are you sure that you bought it at this store?

Customer: What? I bought it from the young man over there yesterday!

Manager: Without the receipt, I can't....

Customer: Wait a minute. Let me see....

(3   )

Manager: That's good. Did you test the CD player before you left the store?

Customer: Test it? No, it was new in the box. (4   )
It was expensive. It's a good brand.

Manager: Of course it is. (5   )

Customer: Come on! I never thought a new CD player wouldn't work.
Do something for me! Give me my money back or give me another
one.

Manager: Take it easy. I'll check it. Hmm....

(6   )

Customer: Yes.

Manager: It's on AC and it should be on DC. Did you read the instructions?

Customer: Oh!

— 5 —

(注)　turn〜on　〜の電源を入れる　　　receipt　レシート
　　　AC　交流　　　DC　直流　　　instructions　使用説明書

問1　本文中の（　1　）〜（　6　）に入る最も適当な文を，次の**ア〜ク**の中から
　　一つずつ選び，記号で答えなさい。

　　ア　But it's always a good idea to test it.

　　イ　How much is it?

　　ウ　I believed it would work.

　　エ　It doesn't work.

　　オ　Uh... I don't have it.

　　カ　When did you buy it?

　　キ　Oh, I've found it in my bag.

　　ク　You see this little switch on the back?

問2　次の1〜4の英文は，この会話文の内容に関するものです。それぞれの
　　（　　　）に入る最も適当な語を下の［　　　］の中から選び，適当な形に変え
　　て答えなさい。ただし，使用する語はそれぞれ1回とします。

　　1　The customer has brought the CD player which he bought at the
　　　store, because he thought it was (　　　).

　　2　The customer gets a little (　　　) after the manager says, "Are you
　　　sure that you bought it at this store?"

　　3　The manager has soon (　　　) out why the CD player doesn't work.

　　4　The customer has (　　　) to read the instructions.

　　　　［　break　carry　excite　find　forget　］

— 6 —

6 次の〔A〕〔B〕をよく読んで，それぞれの問題の指示に従って答えなさい。

〔A〕

Have you ever heard a story like this? A woman moves to a new town with her cat. After a few weeks, her old neighbors are surprised to find the cat at their door. It has found its own way back home.

Not many animals have traveled as far as Tom, a dog in Australia who traveled 1,600 kilometers to come back home. In 1991, Sam, a cat in America, traveled 800 kilometers more than Tom. In Japan, Taro, a dog, traveled half the distance Sam traveled. Do they have maps, a compass or a GPS in their heads?

Scientists believe that cats have something magnetic inside their bodies. They also believe that 'homing' pigeons also have the same thing. They are called 'homing' pigeons because they are always able to find their way home. Many birds travel a long distance without getting lost when they fly south for the winter. They follow the magnetic lines of the earth to find their way.

(注) neighbor 隣人   distance 距離   compass 方位磁石
      GPS 全地球測位システム   magnetic 磁気を帯びた
      homing pigeon 伝書バト   get lost 迷う

(問題) 次の各問いに対する最も適当な答えをア〜エの中から一つずつ選び，記号で答えなさい。

1 How far did the dog, Taro, travel to come back home?

ア 400 kilometers.   イ 800 kilometers.
ウ 1,200 kilometers.   エ 1,600 kilometers.

2 What do homing pigeons use to find their way?

ア Maps in their heads.   イ A compass.
ウ A GPS.   エ The magnetic lines.

〔B〕

Port Washington News

Monday, February 1, 2010

Classified Ads

2-HOUR Weekend English Lessons at Nassau College!	English Lessons in Your Home!
From 8:00 to 20:00. $40 for one lesson. Need to buy a textbook with 2 CDs for $40 at the first lesson. Only 2 to 4 students in a class! Call 735-7849. You can now get a textbook 50% off until the end of March, 2010. Call today!	We have many good teachers in town. $25 for 1 lesson (1 hour each). We can teach on Mondays, Wednesdays, Fridays, and Saturdays from 7:00 to 23:00. Call Hutchinson (714-8181) today and get a 2-hour FREE lesson (Last chance! Until March 31, 2010).

(問題)　上の案内広告(classified ads)に合うように，次の1，2の問いに対する最も適当な答えを**ア〜エ**の中から一つずつ選び，記号で答えなさい。また，3の**ア〜エ**の英文のうち，案内広告の内容を正しく表しているものを一つ選び，記号で答えなさい。

1　How much is 20 hours of lessons at Nassau College before March 31, 2010?

　ア　$420　　　**イ**　$440　　　**ウ**　$820　　　**エ**　$840

2　How much is 10 English lessons on Wednesdays until the end of March?

　ア　$200　　　**イ**　$225　　　**ウ**　$250　　　**エ**　$275

3　**ア**　8-hour lessons at Hutchinson are more expensive than those of Nassau College until the end of March 31, 2010.

　イ　A student can take a 3-hour lesson for $120 at Nassau College on Thursdays.

　ウ　Both Nassau College and Hutchinson give English lessons on Saturdays.

　エ　A student can get a free lesson by calling 735-7849 before March 31, 2010.

7 次の文章はクモ（spider）に関するものです。よく読んで，後の問いに答えなさい。

A spider is a small animal with eight legs. Spiders are best known for the thread they make. They use their thread to catch large and small insects for food.

Many spiders make webs with their threads. They use the webs as traps. 【　A　】 For example, one kind of spider jumps on an insect and eats it. Another spider uses its thread like a line which people use to catch fish. It moves the line until it catches an insect.

Spiders lay eggs. Some large spiders lay 2,000 eggs at a time. One small spider lays just one egg. Many spiders die soon after they lay their eggs. So the babies must learn to take care of themselves.

A lot of people are afraid of spiders, but only a few spiders can hurt humans. In fact, they help us a lot. They kill many bad insects.

A tarantula is a kind of spider. It is large and some are as long as 30cm. It has a lot of hair. People believe that they will become sick if a tarantula bites them, but this is not true. You can find tarantulas in many warm areas such as the American Southwest. American tarantulas live very quietly. These spiders cannot hurt you any more than a bee can.

Some spiders are very dangerous. The black widow is one of these spiders. Its name comes from its color. Its bite will give you much pain. The bite can make you sick for a long time. Only the female black widow can hurt you. She is as small as 1cm long. If you turn her over, you can see something red or yellow on her body. But don't try to turn this spider over!

You can find black widows in almost every state in America. She often makes her webs in dark corners. 【　B　】 She will take a bite at you only when you make her angry.

(注) thread 糸　　insect 昆虫　　web クモの巣　　trap わな
　　　　lay （卵を）産む　　bite かむ／かむこと　　bee ハチ
　　　　pain 痛み　　female メスの　　turn～over ～をひっくり返す

問 1　本文中の下線部の英文が表す内容に最も近いものを次の**ア～エ**の中から一

つ選び，記号で答えなさい。

ア　このクモは，ハチと同じように人を傷つける。

イ　このクモは，人を傷つけることは全くないが，ハチは人を傷つける。

ウ　このクモは，ハチほどには人を傷つけることはない。

エ　このクモは，ハチよりも人を傷つける。

問 2　本文中の【　A　】と【　B　】に入る文を次の**ア～エ**の中から一つずつ選

び，記号で答えなさい。

ア　This spider will not often hurt you.

イ　There are some spiders which help us a lot.

ウ　Making webs is not difficult for them.

エ　But some spiders do not make webs to catch insects.

問 3　本文の内容と合うように，次の1～4の下線部に入るものをそれぞれ下の

ア～エの中から一つずつ選び，記号で答えなさい。

1　Spiders _____

　ア　are small insects with a lot of hair and always lay many eggs.

　イ　use thread to catch not only insects but also fish for food.

　ウ　are very useful to humans because they eat bad insects.

　エ　lay eggs and take care of their babies after they are born.

2　A tarantula _____

　ア　is a large spider with a lot of hair on its body.

　イ　is found in the cool areas like the American Southwest.

　ウ　is very dangerous but people usually don't believe that.

　エ　often makes its webs in dark places.

3　The female black widow _____

　ア　catches an insect by jumping on it and eats it.

　イ　is as large as a tarantula.

　ウ　is known to live in all states in America.

　エ　lives in dark places and can hurt people.

4　To catch an insect, some spiders use _____

　ア　their long legs and move them.

　イ　their thread and move it.

　ウ　their webs and move them.

　エ　their thread and turn it over.

解 答 例 と 解 説

《解答例》

1 (1)ウ (2)エ (3)イ (4)ウ (5)ア

2 1．ウ 2．イ 3．ア 4．ア 5．エ

3 問1．(1)ウ (2)イ (3)ウ (4)エ (5)ア (6)ウ 問2．イ，オ

4 ［3番目／5番目］ 1．［エ／カ］ 2．［ウ／オ］
3．［オ／カ］ 4．［カ／イ］ 5．［ア／カ］

5 1．エ 2．イ 3．ウ 4．イ 5．ウ

6 問1．イ 問2．ア 問3．ウ 問4．ウ 問5．イ
問6．ア 問7．イ

《解　説》

1 (1) 上の文「植物や動物は生きるために水が必要である」，下の文「植物や動物は水なしでは生きられない」
・cannot A without B「BなしにはAできない」

(2) 上の文「この城は400年前に建てられた」，下の文「この城は築400年だ」上の文は（　A　）の直前に be 動詞の was があるので，〈be 動詞＋過去分詞〉の受け身の文にする。

(3) 上の文「トムはあまりに強いので，重い箱を運ぶことができる」，下の文「トムは重い箱を運べるほど十分に強い」
〈so＋ ^{形容詞} 〜 ＋that＋主語＋can/could＋ ^{動詞の原形} …〉
「あまりに〜なので，…できる」の文は，〈 ^{形容詞} 〜 ＋enough to＋ ^{動詞の原形} …〉
「…するほど十分に〜」に書き換えることができる。

(4) 上の文「私は下手なコックだ」，下の文「私は上手に料理することができない」 ・poor cook「下手なコック」

(5) 上の文「もし急がなければ，あなたは最終バスに乗り遅れるでしょう」，下の文「急ぎなさい，さもないとあなたは最終バスに乗り遅れるでしょう」下の文は〈 〜 ＋，or＋…〉「〜しなさい，さもないと…」で，接続詞ifを使った文に書き換えることができる。
・miss＋乗り物「(乗り物に)乗り遅れる」

2 1 A「すみません。市立図書館はどこか私に教えてくれませんか？」
B「ごめんなさい。私はちょうどここを訪問しているだけです」
A「おぉ，わかりました。ウ誰か他の人に尋ねます」

2 A「こんにちは。こちらはジョンです。田中先生をお願いします」
B「ごめんなさい。彼は今ここにいません。イ伝言を預かりましょうか？」
A「はい，お願いします。先生に私は学校に遅れると伝えていただけますか？」 ・take a message「伝言を受け取る／預かる」

3 A「これが，私が君のために東京で買ったTシャツだよ」
B「ありがとう。東京のどこでそれを買ったの？」
A「原宿だよ。ア君はそこに行ったことがある？」
B「一度だけね。通りに沿って歩いて買い物を楽しんだよ」
・Have you ever been to〜？「〜へ行ったことがありますか？」

4 A「私たちは，今週の日曜日に泳ぎに行く予定なの。あなたも来る？」
B「ありがとう，でも今週末は忙しいんだよ」 A「それは残念。
ア次の日曜日はどう？」 B「いいよ。弟を連れて行ってもいいかな？」
A「いいわよ」 ・How about 〜？「〜はいかがですか？」

5 A「午後からリサの誕生日パーティーを開催するの。手伝ってくれない？」 B「いいよ，お母さん。何をすればいい？」 A「テーブルの上にカップを置いてくれない？」 B「いいよ。エいくつ必要？」

A「6個よ」

3 問1 【3 本文の要約】参照。(1) 主語が rockets で，「使われる」という意味の受け身の文にするので，ウ be used が適切。 (2) 直後に trying があるので，「挑戦し続けた」という意味の文になるイ kept が適切。 ・keep 〜ing「〜し続ける」 (3) 直前に be 動詞 was があり，その後の内容から「ショックを受けた」という意味の受け身の文にするので，ウ shocked が適切。 (4) 後ろに than があるので，much「たくさん」の比較級 more が適切。

(5) （ 5 ）の前 a new kind of rocket「新種のロケット」，後ろ used a special fuel「特殊な燃料を使った」より，後ろの内容が前の内容の説明になっているので，関係代名詞のア that が適切。

(6) 特定の日付や曜日の前には，前置詞の on を使うので，ウが適切。

問2 ○については【3 本文の要約】参照。ア×「ゴッダードは高校生の時，武器としての花火を勉強した」…本文にない内容。

イ○「ゴッダードは大学生の時，最初のロケットを作った」

ウ「ゴッダードは大学を卒業した後，×高校の先生になった」…ゴッダードは大学の先生になったので誤り。

エ「ゴッダードは×月へ飛行することができるロケットを作った最初の男だ」…ゴッダードが作ったのは 12mの高さまで飛ぶロケットだから誤り。

オ○「アメリカの新聞は，ゴッダードが亡くなった後に，彼の考えは正しかったという記事を載せた」

【3 本文の要約】

ロバート・ゴッダードはロケットでの月への飛行が可能だと信じていた最初のアメリカ人科学者の一人であった。ロバート・ゴッダードが生まれる前は，ロケットは花火あるいは戦争の兵器としてしか使われていなかった。ほとんどの科学者はロケットが宇宙飛行に 問1(1)使われる(＝be used) ことが可能などとは考えていなかった。

ロバート・ゴッダードは高校生の時，宇宙旅行へのロケットの使用を考え始めた。彼は 1904 年に高校を卒業し，問2イ大学生の時に最初のロケットを作った。それは飛ばなかったが，彼は挑戦し 問1(2)続けた(＝kept)。

彼は猛勉強し，大学の先生になった。ある日，彼は自分のアイディアについてのレポートを書いた。そのレポートで，彼はロケットはいつの日か月へ飛行が可能となるだろうと述べた。しかし，1920 年，彼はニューヨークタイムズ紙に載った話を読んで 問1(3)ショックを受けた(＝shocked)。その話というのは，ゴッダードは間違っていて，ロケットは決して宇宙へは飛行できないというものだった。それには高校生でさえ科学についてゴッダードより 問1(4)もっと多く(＝more) 知っているとも書かれていた。

ゴッダードは腹を立て，もっと性能の良いロケットを作ろうとより熱心に研究した。彼は特別な燃料を使用した 問1(5)(＝関係代名詞の that)新種のロケットを作りたいと考えた。ついに，1926 年3月16 問1(6)に(＝on) 彼の新しいロケットは 12 メートルの高さまで飛んだ。

ゴッダードは月まで飛行できるロケットは作らなかったが，多くの素晴らしいアイディアを考えた。彼は 1945 年に亡くなった。後に科学者たちはより大きくそして性能の良いロケットを作るために彼のアイディアを使った。1969 年に初めて人類が月面を歩いた時，問2オニューヨークタイムズ紙はついにゴッダードの考えは正しかったという記事を載せた。

4 1 I heard the pictures painted on the walls are also beautiful.：「壁に描かれた絵もまた美しいそうです」

「壁に描かれた絵」は〈painted＋on the walls〉で後ろから直前の名詞（＝ここでは pictures）を修飾して表す。
・I heard（that）～「～だそうです」

2 Walking for more than twenty minutes every day is good for our health.：「毎日 20 分以上のウォーキングは私たちの健康によい」every day までが主語の文になる。for は後ろに時間を表す語句がくると「～の間」の意味になる。　・more than ～「～以上」

3 Will you give me something hot to drink?：「私に何かあたたかい飲み物をいただけませんか？」something の位置に注意する。「何かあたたかい飲み物」という表現のように，something を形容詞と to 不定詞で修飾するときは，〈something＋形容詞＋to＋動詞の原形〉の語順にする。　・give＋人＋物「（人）に（物）を与える」

4 Which train will arrive at Yokohama before noon ?：「どの列車が正午前に横浜に到着しますか？」
・Which train～?「どの列車が～？」　・arrive at「～に到着する」

5 How long does it take from here to the city museum by taxi ?
：「タクシーでここから市立美術館までどれくらいの時間がかかりますか？」・How long does it take ~?「～にどれくらいの時間がかかる？」
・from A to B「AからBまで」

5 1 「タカシの母と姉が見た映画は（　）です」…第2段落でタカシの家族は4時半に映画館に着き，母と姉は映画が始まるまで約 30 分間待っていたので，タイトルと上映時間の表より，17：05 に始まるエ Jack the Rabbit が適切。

2 「タカシの家族は映画を見るのに（　）使いました」…特別料金の表に着目する。タカシの家族が映画を見に行ったのは金曜日だから，女性2名（母と大学生の姉）の料金はそれぞれ 1100 円である。また，基本料金の表より，父は 1800 円，中学生のタカシは 1000 円だから，1100×2＋1800＋1000＝5000（円）となる。したがってイが適切。

3 「タカシは家に帰る前に，母と姉を約（　）分待ちました」…第2段落でタカシと父が見た映画は，16：30 に映画館に到着した数分後に始まったので，タイトルと上映時間の表より，16：35 から始まった The Robot War か The World of Animals のどちらかである。これらの映画はともに 18：20（18：40 に終わる母と姉が見た映画よりも 20 分早い）に終わるので，タカシは母と姉を約 20 分（＝20 minutes）待ったと考えられる。したがってウが適切。

4 「マユミの家族は映画を見るのに（　）使いました」…第3段落の最後の文参照。マユミの父がインターネットでチケットを予約しているので，インターネット予約特別料金の表より，大人2名（父と母）の料金がそれぞれ 1500 円になる。中学生のマユミは 1000 円，小学生の妹は 800 円だから，1500×2＋1000＋800＝4800（円）となる。したがってイが適切。

5 「マユミが見た映画は（　）です」…第3段落参照。タカシがマユミに自分が見た映画について話し，それを聞いたマユミはわくわくして映画を見たくなったので，タカシとマユミは同じ映画を見たと考えられる。3の解説より，タカシが見た映画は The Robot War か The World of Animals である。タイトルと上映時間の表より，マユミの家族が映画を

見た午前中に上映されているのは The World of Animals である。したがってウが適切。

【5 本文の要約】
タカシは中学生です。彼は両親と姉と一緒に住んでいます。彼の姉は大学生です。マユミはタカシのクラスメイトです。彼女は彼の家のとなりに住んでいます。マユミにも妹がいます。彼女は小学生です。この2つの家族は映画がとても好きです。

ある金曜日の午後，タカシの家族は映画館へ行きました。彼らは4時半にそこへ着き，見る映画を選びました。タカシと父の映画はあと数分で始まるので，彼らはチケットを買うために急ぎました。彼らが座席に座るとすぐ，映画は始まりました。タカシの姉は別の映画を選び，母もそれを気に入りました。彼女たちはチケットを買い，映画が始まるまで約 30 分間待っていました。家族は映画を楽しんだ後，一緒に家に帰りました。

次の朝，タカシはマユミに会って，父と一緒に見た映画について話しました。彼女はそれを聞いてとてもわくわくし，その映画を見たいと思いました。それから彼女は父に映画館へ連れて行ってくれるよう頼みましたが，父はその日は歯医者に行かなければならないと言いました。それで，彼女たちはその次の日に映画に行くことに決めました。彼女の母と妹も彼女たちに加わりたいと言いました。彼女の父はインターネットで家族の4枚の映画のチケットを予約しました。

次の朝，マユミの家族は映画を見に行きました。彼女たちは映画をとても楽しみました。そのあと彼女たちは昼食を食べ，買い物に行きました。

6 問1 【6 本文の要約】参照。イ「彼らはパンを作るために，太陽からのエネルギーを使った」が適切。ア「太陽に似ているパンを作った」，ウ「彼らは旅行し，たくさんの場所でパンを作った」はいずれも前後の内容と合わない。　・look like ～「～に似ている」

問2 【6 本文の要約】参照。1 の直前の1文で，「Com は古い言葉で "with" を表し，panis は古い言葉で "bread" を表す」とあることから，ア「a person with bread」が companion の意味として最も適切。

問3 【6 本文の要約】参照。2 の前後の内容から判断する。直前の1文「しかし現代では多くの人が昼食時には職場や学校にいる」と，直後の1文「彼らは午後8時ごろに夕食のテーブルについて食事をし，1，2時間話をする」より，ウ「軽めの昼食としっかりした夕食をとっている」が適切。

問4 【6 本文の要約】参照。

問5 【6 本文の要約】参照。3 の直前の1文「例えばイギリスでは，朝食と昼食の間に "elevenses" と呼ばれる軽食を食べる」より，イ「仕事を中断し，紅茶を飲み，パンやケーキを食べる」が適切。
・stop ~ing「～するのをやめる／中断する」

問6 【6 本文の要約】参照。4 の前後の内容から判断する。4 の前後で，農場での収穫時の食事について書かれているので，ア「農場で働く家族は少なくなっている」が適切。

問7 ○については【6 本文の要約】参照。ア×「アメリカの家族はもはや伝統的な収穫時のごちそうを食べない」…最終段落の内容に反する。　イ○「家族の食事の伝統はどの国でも重要である」　ウ×「人々は長い間働くので，食事のために伝統的な時間を持っている」…本文に

ない内容。

6 本文の要約

およそ5,000年前，エジプトの人々は小麦粉と水でパンを作った。問1彼らは太陽の熱でパンを焼いた。彼らが旅に出る時は，パンを持って行った。他の地域の人々もまたパン作りを学んだ。パンは多くの地域で重要な食物となった。

友人とパンや他の食べ物を分け合うのは古くからの伝統である。この伝統は「breaking bread」と呼ばれている。「companion」という言葉（他の言葉では「friend」）は我々にこの伝統について伝えている。Comは古い言葉で「with」を表し，panisは古い言葉で「bread」を表す。つまりcompanionとは 問2. 1ア パンを持った人 で，友人である。

問7イ どの国でも，家族との食事は大切な伝統である。しかし，現代では人々は多忙なことが多く，いつも家族と食事をすることができるとは限らない。昔，フランスでは一日のうちのしっかりした食事は昼食であった。しかし現代では多くの人が昼食時には職場や学校にいる。それで，今では 問3. 2ウ 多くの家庭は軽めの昼食としっかりした夕食をとっている。彼らは午後8時ごろに夕食のテーブルについて食事をし，1，2時間話をすることが多い。

問4③. A しかしながらスペインでは，多くの店や会社は昼食のために閉まる。 →問4②. B それで，家族は一緒にしっかりした昼食を食べることができる。 →問4①. C 彼らはかなり遅い時間の午後9時ごろに軽めの夕食を食べる。

いくつかの国では，軽食のための伝統的な時間がある。例えばイギリスでは，朝食と昼食の間に「elevenses」と呼ばれる軽食を食べる。今でも11時に 問5. 3イ 仕事を中断し，紅茶を飲み，パンやケーキを食べる 人がいる。

スペイン語で「eleven」はonceと言う。チリではonceと呼ばれる軽食がある。人々はパン，肉，ケーキを食べ，紅茶かコーヒーを飲み，友人と話す。しかし，チリの人々は午前11時にonceを食べない。彼らは午後5時ごろにそれを食べる。

昔は，多くの家族が農場で働いていた。休日や収穫時には彼らは「feasts」を食べた。「feast」は家族や友人たちと一緒に食べるとても豪華な食事である。今日では 問6. 4ア 農場で働く家族は少なくなっている が，アメリカやカナダでは，今だに伝統的な収穫時のごちそうがある。

2018（平成30）年度　解答例と解説

《解答例》

1　(1)ウ　(2)ア　(3)イ　(4)エ　(5)ア　(6)イ　(7)エ　(8)イ
　　(9)ア　(10)ウ

2　1．ウ　2．イ　3．ア　4．エ　5．イ

3　問1．(1)ウ　(2)イ　(3)イ　(4)エ　(5)ア　(6)イ
　　問2．1．カ　2．ア

4　[3番目／5番目]　1．[オ／ア]　2．[ウ／ア]
　　3．[イ／ウ]　4．[イ／ア]　5．[イ／オ]

5　1．ア　2．ウ　3．イ　4．ウ　5．ア

6　問1．ウ　　問2．ア　　問3．イ　　問4．ア　　問5．イ
　　問6．ウ　　問7．ウ

《解説》

2　1　Aが How often do you go to the library?「あなたはどのくらいの頻度で図書館へ行きますか？」と尋ねたから，ウ「2週間に一度くらいです」が適切。

　2　AとBの最初の発言から，最後のBの発言，I am going to use it this afternoon.「今日の午後にそれ（＝自転車）を使うつもりです」は，BがAに自転車を使ってはいけないと言った理由だとわかる。したがって，イ「どうしてだめなのですか？」が適切。Why not?にはもう一つの意味「（誘いに対して）もちろん」もあるので覚えておこう。

　3　直後にBが The earliest one comes at 7:45.「一番早いバスは7時45分に来ます」と言ったから，時を尋ねるア「次のバスはいつ来ますか？」が適切。

　4　直前にAが Shall we check our answers together?「一緒に答えを確認しましょうか？」と言ったから，エ「はい，そうしましょう」が適切。Shall we ~?「（一緒に）～しましょうか？」という誘いに乗る場合はYes, let's.と答える。

　5　AとBのやりとりから，Aの最後の発言，I met her in the teachers' room yesterday.「昨日職員室で彼女（＝新しい数学の先生）に会いました」は，that lady が新しい数学の先生であると，Aが知っている理由である。したがって，イ「どうして知っているの？」が適切。

3　問1　【3 本文の要約】参照。
　問2　1　「地面で，足をもう一方の足より前に出すことで動く」＝カ「歩く」　・by ~ing「～することによって」　・in front of ~「～の前に」
　　　2　「何かを正しいと思う」＝ア「信じる」　・think that＋主語＋動詞「～だと思う」

[3 本文の要約]

エイミー・ヴァン・ダイケンは子どもの頃病気でした。彼女は喘息を患っていました。喘息患者はうまく呼吸ができないときがあります。エイミーは子どもの頃，何度も病院に通っていました。それで他の子どもができることができませんでした。彼女の担当医が，喘息には水泳がよいと信じていました。(1)それで，エイミーは水泳を始め，それが好きになりました。最初，エイミーは(2)速く泳ぐことができず，レースに参加するといつもビリでした。水泳は彼女にとってとてもきついものでしたが，彼女は(3)決して挑戦をやめ(3)ませんでした。数年後，彼女は前より速く泳げるようになりました。13歳の時にレースに(4)勝ち始めました。高校や大学の頃には，彼女はアメリカで最も速い競泳選手の1人になりました。

1996年にオリンピックがやってくると，エイミーは5つの競技に参加し，4つの金メダルを獲得しました！彼女は1回のオリンピックで4つの

金メダルを獲得した初めてのアメリカ人女性になりました。次の2000年のオリンピックでは，(5)さらに2つの金メダルを獲得しました。

2014年6月，エイミーは脊髄に損傷を与える事故でけがをしました。事故の後，彼女は両脚の感覚を失いました。エイミーは二度と歩けないだろうと，多くの人が思いました。しかし，彼女はあきらめませんでした。2014年8月，彼女は歩行器を使って歩けるようになりました。

エイミーの話は今も多くの人々，特に喘息患者や脊髄損傷を抱える患者を(6)勇気づけています。

4　1　... and I will have to take care of my little sister. : ・will「～だろう」・have to ~「～しなければならない」・take care of ~「～の世話をする」
文意「私は妹の世話をしなければならないでしょう」

　2　Thank you for inviting me to the concert. : ・Thank you for ~ing「～してくれてありがとう」・invite＋人＋to ~「（人）を～に招待する」
文意「私をコンサートに招待してくれてありがとうございます」

　3　..., but you should be careful to get on the right bus. : ・be careful to ~「～するよう気をつける」
文意「…正しいバスに乗るよう気をつけるべきです」

　4　I want to see the pictures you took there. : Aが最初に北海道を旅行したと発言しているから，「私は，あなたがそこ（＝北海道）で撮った写真を見たいです」とすればよい。〈（省略された関係代名詞）＋you took there〉が pictures を修飾して「あなたがそこで撮った写真」を表す。want you to see the pictures「あなたにその写真を見てほしい」は返事として通じないし，pictures の後に took there はつながらないから×。

　5　How about buying this shirt for Mom's birthday? : ・How about ~ing?「～してはどう？」・for one's birthday「～の誕生日に（向けて）」
文意「お母さんの誕生日にこのシャツを買うのはどう？」

5　1　「タカシの家は地図の ア A だ」…サクラ中学校へ行く途中に，ヒバリ小学校があるAが適切。

　2　「サユリの家は地図の ウ C だ」…サユリの妹はまっすぐ進んでヒバリ小学校に行くから，サユリの家はAかCにしぼられる。1の問題より，Aはタカシの家だから，サユリの家はCである。

　3　「サユリは7時20分に家を出て学校に向かえば，イ 7時35分 着く」…右図参照。タカシの家からサクラ中学校までは20分，タカシの家からヒバリ小学校までは15分かかるから，サクラ中学校からヒバリ小学校までは5分かかる。したがって，サユリの家からサクラ中学校まで行くのにかかる時間は20－5＝15(分)である。

各地点までの移動にかかる時間（単位：分）
Hはヒバリ小学校，Sはサクラ中学校を表す

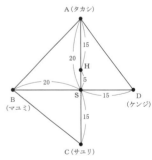

　4　「タカシはケンジの家に行った時，ウ 10時25分 に着いた」…1・2の問題より，ケンジの家はBかDにしぼられる。ケンジの家からサクラ中学校まで15分，サユリの家からサクラ中学校まで20分だから，ケンジの家はサクラ中学校までの距離が短いDである。
移動にかかる時間は〔距離÷速さ〕で求められるから，最初にADの距離を求めて，その後速さで割る。ADの距離は，三平方の定理を使い，$AD^2 = AS^2 + DS^2$ で求められる。問題文より，登場人物全員の歩く速度は一定だから，速度をxとして考えると，$AS = 20x$，$DS = 15x$だ

から，ＡＤ＝$\sqrt{(20x)^2+(15x)^2}$＝25xである。したがって，移動する時間は25x÷x＝25(分)である。なお，3辺の比が3：4：5の直角三角形があるから，3：4：5＝15x：20x：ＡＤとしてＡＤの距離を求めてもよい。

5　「マユミは友達とテニスをするために，｜ア12時55分｜に家を出た」
…ケンジの家からサクラ中学校まで15分で行けるから，タカシとケンジがサクラ中学校に着いたのは午後1時15分である。
マユミの家からサクラ中学校までは20分かかるから，マユミは家を，
1時15分−20分＝12時55分に出た。

【5】本文の要約

タカシ，ケンジ，サユリ，マユミはサクラ中学校の同級生です。

タカシにはヒバリ小学校に通う弟がいます。タカシは毎朝弟と一緒に家を出ます。なぜなら，弟の学校はタカシの学校の途中にあるからです。学校へ行くのに，タカシは20分歩き，弟は15分歩きます。

ケンジは，登校するためにいつも7時35分に家を出て，7時50分に着きます。

サユリにはタカシの弟と同じ学校に通う妹がいます。妹は家から学校までまっすぐ進み，(着くのに)20分かかります。

マユミは，登校するためにいつも7時30分に家を出て，彼女はタカシと同じ時間(＝20分)歩きます。

ある日曜日，タカシはケンジと新しいテレビゲームをするために彼の家に行きました。彼は10時に家を出ました。午後1時に，2人はケンジの家を出ました。学校(＝サクラ中学校)でテニスをする予定があったからです。2人の女子はそれぞれの家から来ました。男子が学校に着くと，女子もちょうど同じ時刻に着きました。

6　【6】本文の要約　参照。
問1　Lots of American people watch birds.と対比される文を入れる。鳥については They do interesting things.とあるが，石については Stones don't do interesting things.とあるから，ウが適切。・few＋○○　～「～する○○はほとんどない」

問2・問3　第1段落で，石について They just lie there.とあるが，第2段落では They didn't just lie there とあるから，問2はアが，問3はイが適切。・by oneself「ひとりで」

問4　｜　4　｜の後に2人の学者が石を観察した具体的な方法が書かれているから，アが適切。

問5　｜　5　｜の2文後に，several stones moved away from their stakes.とある。石が動いたとわかるのは，杭が，もともとの石の位置を示していたからである。したがって，イが適切。

問6　石がひとりで動く仕組みを示した文が入る。石は風で動くが，摩擦が大きいため，そのままでは動かない。地表に氷が張り，摩擦が小さくなることによって，風で動くという流れを読み取る。

問7　○は【6】本文の要約　参照。ア「学者は×21世紀になって初めて石が動いたことを認識した」　イ「1972年から1979年まで，×カレンと名付けられた石は201m動いた」　ウ○「石によってできた通った跡を見たから，人々は石が動いたと考えた」

【6】本文の要約

多くのアメリカ人がバードウォッチングをします。それは容易に理解できます。鳥は美しく，興味深い行動をするからです。しかし，アメリカでは，｜1ウ石を見る人はほとんどいません｜。それも容易に理解できます。石は興味深い行動をしないからです。ただそこにあるだけです。しばらく見ていれば，それがつまらないことだとわかるでしょう。

しかし，カリフォルニアの砂漠地帯にある石の集団においては，｜2ア事態が変わります｜。そこの石は不思議な行動をしたのです。ただそこにあるだけでなく，｜3イひとりでに動いたのです｜。

かつて，その砂漠には湖がありました。その湖はずっと前に干上がってしまいました。今やその土地は固く平らになり，石がそこにあるだけです。

問7ウ石がひとりでに動くことができるとは，誰も思いません。しかし，この石が実際に通った長い跡があったのです。多くの人がその通った跡を見てきました。

なぜその石が動いたか，誰にもわかりませんでした。それは何かを探していたのでしょうか？遊んでいたのでしょうか？石が意志を持って動いたと思う人はほとんどいません。冬には砂漠に少し氷が張ります。その氷が石を動かしたと考えた人がいました。

それがただの氷だとは思わなかった学者が2人いました。そのため，1972年，｜4ア彼らはその石を観察し始めました｜。まず，後ろに通った跡がある石を30個選び，それに名前を書きました。ある石はメリー・アン，またある石はルース，大きな石はカレンと名付けられました。それから学者たちは，それぞれの石のそばの地面に金属の杭を打ち込みました。それは｜5イ学者がどこで石を見つけたか｜を示すものでした。彼らは7年間，石を観察しました。その間，杭から離れた石が数個ありました。ナンシーと名付けられた石は201m動きましたが，カレンは同じ場所に留まったままでした。

今，学者たちはなぜ石が動くのかを知っています。それは風のせいです。｜A③時々地表に雨が降ります。｜→｜B①地表の水が寒い冬の夜間に凍ります。｜→｜C②それから，強風が氷上の石を動かします。｜石は風が吹いている間に動きます。風が止むと，石は止まります。これが，学者たちの解明した事実です。

《解答例》

1　(1)ア　(2)イ　(3)イ　(4)ア　(5)ア　(6)ウ　(7)エ　(8)ウ
　　(9)イ　(10)イ

2　1．ウ　2．エ　3．ウ　4．エ　5．ア

3　問1．(1)イ　(2)ウ　(3)エ　(4)ア　(5)エ　(6)ウ
　　問2．1．エ　2．ウ

4　[3番目／5番目]　1．[エ／カ]　　2．[イ／オ]
　　3．[カ／オ]　4．[ウ／イ]　5．[イ／ウ]

5　1．ア　2．ア　3．エ　4．ウ　5．エ

6　問1．ウ　問2．ア　問3．イ　問4．ウ　問5．イ
　　問6．イ　問7．ウ

《解　説》

2　1　Aが「これはあなたのチケットですか？あなたの席のそばの床で見つけたのですが」と言ったから，ウ「それなら私のものだと思います」が適切。

2　Aの2回目の発言，Don't do that.「それはいけません」より，Aの最初の発言と食い違うエ「それを朝に飲んでもいいですか？」が適切。

3　Bが外食するときにパンを選ぶ理由だから，ウ「私はいつも家でご飯を食べます」が適切。

4　Bの最後の発言，I got up late.「起きるのが遅かった」より，エ「今朝は何も食べなかった」が適切。Why not?は相手の誘いを受ける表現として「もちろん」という意味でよく使われるが，ここでは Why didn't you eat anything?「なぜ何も食べなかったの？」が省略された形である。

5　電話での会話。A「ジョン・グリーンさんはいますか？」→B「おお，お前なのか，フレッド？」→A「うん…」→B「ア(ジョン・グリーンは)僕だよ！どうしていたんだ，フレッド？」という感動の場面である。

3　問1　【3本文の要約】参照。

問2　1　「単語を書いたり話したりすることによる意思疎通のシステム」＝「言語」
　2　「少し前に起きたことに関する情報」＝「ニュース」

【3本文の要約】

太鼓は世界中の人々の音楽において大きな役割を果たしている。しかし，アフリカには，太鼓がもっと重要な(1)役割を担っている地域が多い。

問11．前文の played a big part と had an important job はほぼ同じ意味。

何年もの間，アフリカには良い道路が少ししかない地域があった。電話もテレビも少なかったし，メールはなかった。そんな時，人々はどうやってお互いにメッセージを送るのだろうか？どうやってニュースを知るのだろうか？彼らは太鼓を使ったのだ！

この太鼓は『話す太鼓』と呼ばれている。それらはナイジェリアのヨルバ族に使われている。この太鼓は英語を話すことはできない。(2)しかし，ヨルバ語などの言語を話すことはできる。

問12．be able to と can は同じ意味。(　)の前には not が付いているから，(　)の前後の文は相反する内容である。

英語では Hello!や How are you?と言う。ただ好きな風に言えばよい。しかし，ヨルバ語ではそれができない。1つ1つの単語の言い方に(3)気をつ

けなければならない。それは同じ単語に2つ以上の意味があるからだ。その意味は，単語を言ったときの声の(4)高低によって決まる。

ヨルバ語を話すとき，声は上がったり下がったりする。歌っているように聞こえるが，もちろん本当に歌っているわけではない。話しているのだ。

何年にもわたる(5)練習の末，太鼓奏者は太鼓で『話す』ことができるようになる。なぜなら，高い音や低い音を出すために様々な叩き方で太鼓を叩くからだ。そうすれば，太鼓の音調やリズムがその言語の音に合うのだ。このようにして，ヨルバ族は太鼓の『(6)話す』単語の1つ1つを理解できるのである。

問16．太鼓を叩くことで意思疎通をすることをこの段落の1行目で talk と表現している。

4　1　How many hours does it take to fly to Australia?：Bが「約8時間」と答えているから，かかる時間を尋ねる文にする。
how many hours「何時間」を使った it takes＋時間＋to～「～するのに(時間が)かかる」の疑問文。

2　Please don't tell anyone about our meeting today.：「～しないでください」は〈Please don't＋動詞の原形〉で表す。

3　No, I don't know what it looks like.：文中に疑問詞 what が入るから，間接疑問の文である。know の後を〈疑問詞＋主語＋動詞〉の語順にする。・look like ～「～のように見える」

4　I went to one of the most famous places in the world.：one of the＋最上級＋〇〇(名詞)「最も～な〇〇(名詞)の1つ」を使った文。
「～へ行く」は〈go to＋場所〉で表すから，to は最初にくる。

5　So, English isn't the only language we should study then.：Bの1回目の発言に「中国語が最も多くの人に話されている」とあることからも，この文が「だから，そうなると英語は私たちが勉強するべき唯一の言語ではない」という意味になるとわかる。「私たちが勉強するべき言語」は〈(省略された関係代名詞)＋主語＋(助動詞)＋動詞〉で後ろから名詞(ここでは language)を修飾して表す。「唯一の～」＝the only ～

5　1　「タカシのクラスには ア16 人の男子がいる」…クラス全員 36－女子 20＝16(人)

2　「桜中学校の生徒たちは少なくとも ア9 台のタクシーに乗った」
クラス全員 36÷タクシーの乗車可能人数 4＝9(台)

3　「タカシは エD 班である」…表を右のように書き直すとわかりやすい。第4段落より，最初に金閣寺を訪れ，次に銀閣寺以外の場所を訪れたD班である。

	訪れた順番・場所			
	1	2	3	4
A班	金閣寺	銀閣寺	二条城	清水寺
B班	金閣寺	銀閣寺	清水寺	二条城
C班	清水寺	金閣寺	二条城	
D班	金閣寺	清水寺	二条城	銀閣寺
E班	銀閣寺	清水寺	金閣寺	

4　「マユミは ウ清水寺 で昼食を食べた」…マユミの班は昼食の時間にタカシの班(＝D班)と会ったから，2つの班が2番目に訪れた清水寺が適切。

5　「桜中学校の生徒と先生は少なくともホテルの部屋が エ16 部屋必要だった」…男子の部屋と女子の部屋が別れていることに注意しよう。人数を1部屋にあるベッドの数で割れば必要な部屋の数がわかる。男子に必要な部屋数は 16÷3＝5.333…だから6部屋。女子に必要な部屋数は 20÷3＝6.66…だから7部屋。先生に必要な部屋数は 3÷1＝3だから3部屋。その合計の16部屋が適切。

タカシは桜中学校の生徒です。彼は3年生です。マユミはタカシのクラスメートです。彼女はクラスに20人いる女子の1人です。桜中学校には3年生が1クラスしかなく，そのクラスには36人の生徒がいます。

ある日，桜中学校の3年生が修学旅行で京都へ行きました。3人の先生が一緒に行きました。彼らは新幹線に乗り，9時に京都駅に着きました。

京都駅に着いた後，生徒たちはタクシーで市内を見て回るために，班に分かれました。旅行をする前に，各班は1日目に京都市内の少なくとも3か所を訪れる計画を立てました。1台のタクシーは4人の乗客を乗せることができました。先生たちは市内をバスで回りました。

タカシの班は最初に金閣寺を訪れました。次の場所では銀閣寺から来たマユミの班に会いました。彼らは一緒に昼食を食べました。

17時30分，生徒全員と先生たちがホテルに集合しました。男子の部屋は2階に，女子の部屋は3階にありました。生徒用の部屋には1部屋に3つのベッドがあり，先生用の部屋には1部屋に1つのベッドがありました。

6 問1～4 【6本文の要約】参照。

問5 ○は【6本文の要約】参照。ア「それはニューオーリンズ市を襲い，×1250億ドルの損害をもたらした」

イ○「それは2005年の11番目のハリケーンで，ニューオーリンズ市に損害を与えた」…Kは英語のアルファベットで11番目である。

ウ×「ニューオーリンズ市の人々が覚えたいから，それは彼らによって名づけられた」

問6 Walterの頭文字Wは英語のアルファベットで23番目だが，それより前のアルファベットであるQとUがないから，イが適切。

問7 ○は【6本文の要約】参照。ア「サンタアナは×20世紀にプエルトリコを襲った嵐だった」 イ×「アメリカの人々は恐ろしいハリケーンにちなんで都市に名前をつける」 ウ○「2012年のハリケーン・サンディーはハリケーン・カトリーナよりも大きな損害をもたらした」

【6本文の要約】

大きな嵐は世界の地域によって違う名づけられ方をする。日本では台風と呼ばれ，1番号が与えられる。しかしアメリカでは，大きな嵐はハリケーンと呼ばれ，『ウィリアム』や『エミリー』などの名前がつけられる。問7ウ2012年，ハリケーン・サンディーはアメリカの多くの都市に損害を与えた。この嵐は1250億ドルの損害をもたらした。なぜそれは『サンディー』と名づけられたのだろうか？

ハリケーンに名前をつけるのは，約200年前に始まった。最初はハリケーン・サンタアナがプエルトリコを襲った1825年だった。後に，アメリカ軍がハリケーンをより覚えやすくするために女性の名前をつけ始めた。1953年，アメリカの国立ハリケーンセンターがハリケーンに名前をつけ始めた。その名前はニュース報道で使われたので，2人々は嵐を簡単に覚えることができた。

現在，男性の名前も女性の名前も大西洋のハリケーン用の6種類のリストに書かれている。1年に1つのリストが使われる。問5最初の嵐の名前は英語のアルファベットで最初の文字『A』から始まる。2つ目の嵐は英語のアルファベットで2番目の文字『B』から始まる名前を与えられる，などだ。しかし，Q，U，X，Y，Zの文字で始まる名前はリストにない。6つのリストすべてが使われた後，再び最初から使われる。

しかし，3多くの都市を襲い大きな損害をもたらすハリケーンもあるので，そういうハリケーンの名前は2度と使われることはない。

問5ハリケーン・サンディーが多くの都市を襲った7年前(＝2005年)，ニューオーリンズ市のほとんどがハリケーン・カトリーナに襲われた。問7ウハリケーン・カトリーナは500億ドルの損害をもたらした。その恐ろしさから，今では多くのアメリカ人がその2つのハリケーンを覚えている。

陸に近づくが何の損害ももたらさずに海へ戻っていくハリケーンもある。そういうことが起きると，人々は4幸運の象徴としてそのハリケーンにちなんだ名前を子どもにつけるときがある。

《解答例》

1 (1)イ (2)ウ (3)イ (4)エ (5)ア (6)エ (7)イ (8)ウ

2 1．ア 2．イ 3．エ 4．イ 5．ウ

3 (1)ウ (2)イ (3)イ (4)エ (5)エ (6)ウ

4 ［3番目／5番目］ 1．［オ／エ］ 2．［ウ／エ］
 3．［イ／ア］ 4．［イ／オ］ 5．［イ／ウ］

5 1．エ 2．イ 3．ウ 4．ウ 5．イ

6 問1．ア 問2．イ 問3．ウ 問4．イ 問5．ウ
 問6．イ 問7．ウ

《解 説》

2 1 直後にBが No, I can't.「いいえ，それはできません」と答えたから，yes/no で答えられるア「もっと速く歩きましょうか？」が適切。

2 直後にBが I do, too.「私もです」と言ったから，時制が現在で肯定文のイ「ええと，ミルクを入れれば好きです」が適切。Yes は常に肯定を表すから，アの Yes, I do.は「私はコーヒーが好きです」という意味になり，次の文と矛盾する。

3 AはBから午後は雨が降りそうだと聞き，サッカーではなく体育館でバレーボールをしようと提案した。ア，イはBがサッカーをすることに前向きな発言だから×。また，let's ~.「～しよう」という提案に Me, too.「私もです」と答えることはできないからウは×。

4 直後にBが Almost every day.「ほぼ毎日です」と答えたから，頻度(回数)を尋ねるイ「あなたはどのくらいの頻度でギターを練習しますか？」が適切。アはギターを演奏している期間，ウは持っているギターの本数，エはギターの演奏の学び方を尋ねる疑問文。

5 直後のBの発言，I had a headache.は「私は頭痛がしました」という意味だから，相手を心配して体調を尋ねるウが適切。

3 (1) 「彼女の両親はとても驚いた」という意味になるから，ウが適切。4歳の娘が一人で家の屋根に登ってしまった両親の気持ちである。
・be surprised「(人)が驚く」・be surprising「驚くべき」

(2) 直前に enjoyed があるから，ing 形のイが適切。・enjoy ~ing「～することを楽しむ」

(3) ・be interested in ~「～に興味がある」

(4) 主語が it で直後に時間を表す言葉があるから，エが適切。
・it takes＋時間「(時間)がかかる」

(5) ( )以下が pilot を修飾するようにするから，to 不定詞のエが適切。

(6) ・the＋副詞の最上級＋of all「すべての中で最も～」なお，前置詞に続く名詞が複数形なら of を使い，単数形なら in を使う。

4 1 It is one of the famous stories written by Natsume Soseki.
：〈過去分詞＋語句〉で後ろから名詞を修飾する文。
・one of＋名詞の複数形「～の1つ」

2 I've used it since I started working five years ago.：3つある動詞(used, started, working)の使い方がポイント。working は started の直後に置いて，started working とする。( )直前に I've があるから，最初は過去分詞。また，( )直後に five years ago とあるから，〈現在

完了の文＋since＋時制が過去の文〉の形。「私は5年前に働き始めてからずっとそれを使っている」という意味の文になる。

3 A scientist wanted to make his father's work easier for him.
：・make A B「A を B(の状態)にする」

4 Do you know where I can buy something cold to drink?：疑問詞が know の後にある間接疑問文だから，疑問詞の後を〈主語＋(助)動詞〉の語順にする。また，something を形容詞と to 不定詞で修飾するときは，〈something＋形容詞＋to＋動詞の原形〉の語順にする。

5 I broke the cup Tom gave me for my birthday.：2つある動詞(broke, gave)の使い方がポイント。( )内に，目的語に〈that＋主語＋動詞〉をとる動詞や関係代名詞，接続詞がないから，目的格の関係代名詞が省略されている文である。

5 読み取った情報を整理する力が試される問題。最初に全体をざっと読み，次に〔B〕の文章から読み取れる情報をまとめてから〔A〕の文章を読み込んでいくと解きやすい。

1 「アキコの母親が買ったケーキには 150 g の砂糖が含まれていた」：ケーキ 100 g には 10 g の砂糖が入っていたから，1500÷100×10＝150(g)となる。

2 「アキコの父親が食べられなかったケーキは 250 g である」：1500 g のケーキを半分に切り，それを3人で均等に分けたから，1500÷2÷3＝250(g)となる。

3 「アキコが飲んだジュースには 25 g の砂糖が含まれていた」：アキコは 500ml 入りのジュースを半分飲み，そのジュースには 100ml あたり 10 g の砂糖が含まれていたから，500÷2÷100×10＝25(g)となる。

4 「アキコの友達は1人 200 g のケーキを食べた」：夜に残っていたケーキは(1500÷2＋250) ［父親の分］ g。それを友達3人とアキコ，母親の5人で均等に分けたから，(1500÷2＋250)÷5＝200(g)となる。

5 「アキコが誕生日に食べたケーキと飲んだジュースには 70 g の砂糖が入っていた」：アキコが食べたケーキの量は上記2と5の合計と同じだから，(250＋200) g。それに入っていた砂糖は 450÷100×10＝45(g)である。飲んだジュースに入っていた砂糖は上記3より 25 g だから，45＋25＝70(g)となる。

【本文の要約】

〔A〕

ある日の午後，その日はアキコの誕生日だったのでアキコの母親はケーキと瓶のジュースを買った。ケーキはとても大きかったので，母親はそれを半分に切った。彼女はその半分を冷蔵庫に入れた。アキコと両親はもう半分を分けて食べた。母親はその(半分の)ケーキを3つに切った。それぞれの大きさは同じだった。ケーキを食べ始めたちょうどその時，父親が電話を受け，会社へ行かなくてはならなくなった。そのため，彼は少しもケーキを食べることができなかった。母親は父親の残したケーキを冷蔵庫に入れた。その後，アキコと母親はそれぞれ瓶のジュースを半分飲んだ。

その夜，アキコの友達のユミコ，トモコ，サオリが彼女の家に来た。アキコは母親に冷蔵庫のケーキを出すよう頼んだ。母親はケーキを全部冷蔵庫から出し，アキコ，友達3人，そして自分用に切った。全員が同じ量のケーキを食べた。アキコの友達は母親が買ったジュースを

飲んだ。しかしアキコと母親は砂糖なしのコーヒーを飲んだ。

〔B〕

　アキコの母親が買ったケーキは 1500 g で，ジュースは瓶 1 本 500ml である。ケーキ 100 g には 10 g の砂糖が含まれていた。ジュース 100ml には 10 g の砂糖が含まれていた。

6　問1　【本文の要約】参照。ニューヨークはロサンゼルスより 3 時間早いから，ニューヨーク時間の午前 8 時は，ロサンゼルス時間では午前 5 時である。

　問2　【本文の要約】参照。時差が発生する原因である。

　問3　【本文の要約】参照。段落全体の内容から，時間と関係の深いウが適切。

　問4　【本文の要約】参照。アメリカをタイムゾーンで分割した下の地図より，ニューヨークはロサンゼルスより 3 時間早いから，8 ＋ 3 ＝ 11(時)が適切。

　問5　【本文の要約】参照。時差が 2 つある州もあることなどから読み取る。

　問6　○は【本文の要約】参照。ア「タイムゾーンは×世界の国々を分割している線である」…下線部は国境の説明だから×。　イ○「タイムゾーンは世界を分割した 24 の地域の 1 つである」　ウ×「アメリカには州境があったからタイムゾーンは発明された」…本文にない内容。

　問7　○は【本文の要約】参照。ア×「日時計と水時計は時間と分を使って時刻を示すために発明された」…本文にない内容。　イ×「何千年も前，だれもが 1 日は 24 時間あると思っていた」…本文にない内容。ウ○「アメリカには時間が異なる州がある」

【本文の要約】

　現在ニューヨークは午後 3 時です。ロサンゼルスは何時ですか？ 正午です。なぜですか？ それはタイムゾーン(＝地域によって標準時が変わること)のせいです。例えば，ニューヨークの生徒は午前 8 時に学校に行きますが，太陽は昇っています。しかし，ロサンゼルスの生徒が同じ時間に登校しなければならないなら，彼らは│1太陽が昇る│前にそうしなければなりません。なぜでしょうか？ それは│2地球が自転している│からです。だから太陽は毎朝昇り，夜には沈みます。地球の太陽の方を向いている部分が昼で，その他の部分が夜です。これは毎日 24 時間変わります。

　常にタイムゾーンがあるとは限りません。何千年もの間，人々は日時計や水時計，あるいは現在時刻を示す他の種類の時計を使っていましたが，だれも分や時間のことを知りませんでした。数百年前，時計や腕時計が発明されましたが，だれも│3タイムゾーンが必要であることを知りませんでした。

　1879 年，サンフォード・フレミングが世界を 24 のタイムゾーンに分割し，その結果アメリカは 4 つのタイムゾーンに分割されました。それぞれのタイムゾーンはその東のタイムゾーンに対して 1 時間遅れています。そのため，ロサンゼルスで午前 8 時なら，ニューヨークでは│4午前 11 時│なのです。

　アメリカを 4 つのタイムゾーンに分割した地図は必ずしも州境に沿っているわけではありません。2 つのタイムゾーンにわたる州もあり

ます。だからそうした州を旅行するときは，2 つの異なる時間を示した時計を目にするかもしれません。これはいったいどういうことを意味するのでしょうか？アメリカを旅行するときは，│5その地域の時間をチェックする必要がある│，ということです。

《解　答》

1 　(1)engineer　(2)missed　(3)global　(4)fourth　(5)information

2 　1．ウ　2．エ　3．ア　4．イ　5．ア

3 　(1)ウ　(2)イ　(3)ウ　(4)イ　(5)エ

4 　[3番目／5番目]　1．[ウ／カ]　2．[ウ／オ]　3．[ア／カ]
　　4．[ア／ウ]　5．[オ／カ]

5 　1．ア　2．ウ　3．イ　4．ウ　5．イ

6 　問1．【A】イ　【B】ウ　問2．ウ　問3．イ
　　問4．1．イ　2．ア　問5．ウ　問6．natural

《解　説》

1 　(1)ア「道路や建物，機械などを設計，建造する人」＝engineer「技師」

　(2)ア「乗り遅れる」イ「〜がいないのを寂しく思う」＝miss

　(3)ア global warming＝「地球温暖化」

　(4)ア April＝4番目の月＝the fourth month of the year

　(5)ア look for information on the Internet＝ネット上の情報を検索する」

2 　1．そのテレビ番組を見たくない理由を答えたウ「ルールがわからない」が適切。

　2．（　）の直後に B が「あと2週間ここにいる」と具体的に答えたから，滞在する期間を尋ねたエが適切。

　3．（　）の直後に B が「トップは長いまま，後ろと両サイドは良い具合に短く」と答えたから，ア「今日，髪はどのようにされますか？」が適切。
　・nice and …「（後ろにくる形容詞を強調して）良い具合に」

　4．（　）の直後に B が「また今度ね！」と答えたから，B の誘いを断るイが適切。

　5．（　）の直後に B が「そうして下さい」と答えたから，ア「彼に電話をさせましょうか？」が適切。エは電話をした人が伝言を頼む表現だから不適切。

3 　【インタビューの要約】参照。(1)・happen「（事が偶然）起きる」

　(2)・because of 〜「〜の理由で」

　(3)remove「取り去る」ここでは「切断する」

　(4)・for 〜「〜に適した，目的にかなった」　(5)work「機能する」

【インタビューの要約】

インタビュアー：今夜は，ヒュー・ハーさんとお話しします。こんばんは，ヒューさん。あなたは事故で両足を失いました。それはどのように[1]起きたのか，お話し下さいますか？

ヒュー・ハーさん：承知しました。私は 1982 年にワシントン山に登っていました。突然，天気がひどく悪くなり，雪が降り始めました。何も見えなくなって道に迷いました。気温はほぼ零下 30 度でした。私は山で4日を過ごしました。食料や設備はありませんでした。発見された時には重体でした。寒さ[2]のため，足を動かすことができませんでした。私は病院に運ばれ，2か月入院しました。入院中，医師は私の両足を[3]切断しました。

インタビュアー：そうでしたか。でもあなたは登山を続けたかったんです

ね。

ヒュー・ハーさん：その通りです。それで私は[4]自分に適した新しい足を作ることにしました。

インタビュアー：それでこのすばらしい新たな足を造られたんですね？

ヒュー・ハーさん：ええ。自分で試してみましたが，この足は本当にうまく[5]動くんです。それに登山靴よりずっとパワフルなんですよ！

インタビュアー：すばらしいですね！

4 　1．Do you like taking care of your sister？「妹の世話をするのは好きですか？」・like 〜ing「〜するのが好き」
　・take care of 〜「〜の世話をする」

　2．Do you know what time her plane will arrive？「彼女の飛行機が何時に到着するか，ご存知ですか？」
　間接疑問の文。〈what time＋主語＋動詞〉の語順になる。

　3．Because we have known each other since we were children．「子どもの頃から知っているからです」
　現在完了「継続」の文。・each other「お互いに」・since＋過去を表す文「〜から」

　4．Can you tell me the shortest way to the station？「駅へ行く一番近い道を教えてくれますか？」

　5．The students Mr. Smith teaches have to make speeches in class.「スミス先生が教える生徒は授業でスピーチをしなければならない」students の直後の関係代名詞 that が省略されていることに注意。・have to 〜「〜しなければならない」・make speech「スピーチをする」

5 　1．午前中にタカシの家族が歌った曲数＝両親1曲＋タカシ1曲＋タカシの弟と妹1曲＋父2曲＋母1曲＝ア．6曲

　2．ジュリーが歌った曲数＝ジュリーと彼女の母が2曲＋ジュリーと彼女の姉のアンが1曲＋ジュリーとタカシが1曲＝ウ．4曲

　3．タカシがその日歌った ABC47 の曲数＝タカシ1曲＋ジュリーの母に歌うよう頼まれた1曲＋ジュリーとタカシが1曲＝イ．3曲

　4．その日カラオケに行った人数＝タカシの家族5人＋ジュリーの家族3人＝ウ．8人

　5．タカシの家族は2時間 20 分いたので，3時間分の料金を支払う。大人2人と中学生1人，小学生2人だから，カラオケの代金は1000×2＋800＝2800（円）　ジュリーの家族は 50 分いたので，1時間分の料金を支払う。大人1人と中学生・高校生2人だから 500＋300×2＝1100（円）。タカシの父は，2家族分のカラオケ料金とピザ大の料金 1000 円を加えた，イ．4900 円を支払った。

【本文の要約】

タカシは中学生です。彼には弟と妹がいます。弟のヒロシは 10 歳，妹のトモコは5歳です。

タカシの家の隣のジュリーも中学生です。彼女は両親，姉と住んでいます。ジュリーの姉のアンは高校生です。

ある日，タカシと家族はカラオケに行きました。彼らは午前 11 時に受付をしました。最初に両親が一緒に1曲歌いました。それからタカシがお

気に入りのグループ，ABC47 の歌を1曲歌いました。次に弟と妹が一緒に子どもの歌を歌いました。その後父が2曲歌い，母が大好きな歌を1曲歌いました。

正午に，お腹がすいたので，ピザの大と飲み物を注文しました。30 分後，ジュリーの家族が同じ場所に来て受付をしました。彼らはタカシの家族に気づいたので合流しました。ジュリーの母は ABC47 の歌が好きですがあまりうまく歌えません。それでタカシに ABC47 の歌の1曲を歌ってほしいと頼んだので，タカシは歌いました。ジュリーの父はその日仕事があり来ませんでした。ジュリーと彼女の母は2曲一緒に歌いました。そしてジュリーはアンと1曲歌いました。彼女がタカシと歌った歌も ABC47 でした。

1時 20 分，2家族は歌い終わり帰宅しました。タカシの父がみんなのカラオケや食べ物の料金を払いました。

6　問1．【本文の要約】参照。

　問2．動物が安心して長く眠れる環境は「動物園にいるとき」である。

　問3．(X)は睡眠時間が1番短い動物…第2段落最後の文参照。ゾウの睡眠時間は約4時間。(Z)は睡眠時間が1番長い動物…第2段落2〜3行目参照。コウモリの睡眠時間は約 20 時間。(Y)の次がトラであることに着目する。第3段落1〜2行目から，ライオンと判断する。従ってイが適当。

　問4．1．第4段落最後の文参照。　2．第3段落参照。

　問5．グラフからイヌの睡眠時間は 11 時間，ネコの睡眠時間は 12 時間，トラが 16 時間。本文から馬の睡眠時間は約4時間だからウが適当。

　問6．natural environment＝「自然環境」

【本文の要約】

　動物の睡眠時間はそれぞれ違う。1日あたりわずかな時間しか眠らない動物もいれば，半日あるいはそれ以上眠る動物もいる。

　この違いには多くの理由がある。おそらく主な理由は動物の大きさであろう。普通，【A】小さな動物は大きな動物より長く眠る。例えば，コウモリのような小さな動物は1日あたり 20 時間眠る。とはいえ，ゾウやキリン，馬のような大きな動物はみな，1日あたり約4時間しか眠らない。

　他にも理由がある。ライオンやトラのように獲物を狩る動物は，他の動物を恐れる必要がないため長く眠る。シカのように（獲物として）狩られる動物は，1日あたりほんのわずかな時間しか眠らない。何時間も寝てしまえば他の動物に捕まるかもしれないからだ。

　動物の年齢も，また別の理由である。人間のように，動物は年齢によって睡眠時間が違う。例えば，若い動物はたいてい，年上の動物より多く眠る必要がある。

　動物は，捕獲され動物園に置かれると睡眠時間も変化する。動物はたいてい野生の状態より動物園にいる方が多く眠る。エサは与えられ，命を脅かす動物からは守られている。問2．それで安心して長く眠ることができる。

　しかし，野生の状態にいる動物は，1日何時間も，狩りやエサ集めをしなければならない。【B】エサを見つけるために，長距離を移動しなければならない動物もいる。危険な動物が近くにいれば警戒もしなければならない。だから動物は，問6．自然環境にいる場合，より少ない時間しか眠らないのかもしれない。

　例えば，動物園にいる動きの遅いナマケモノは，1日あたり 16 時間眠る。ナマケモノを研究するために，科学者の一団が熱帯雨林に行った。彼らは，ナマケモノが問6．自然環境では1日あたり約 10 時間しか眠らないことを発見したのだ。

《解 答》

1 (1)thousand　(2)touch　(3)Saturday　(4)understand
　(5)message

2 1．ウ　2．ア　3．エ　4．イ　5．ア

3 (1)ア　(2)ウ　(3)ウ　(4)エ　(5)ア

4 [3番目, 5番目] 1．[エ, ウ]　2．[オ, ア]　3．[カ, イ]
　4．[イ, エ]　5．[ア, カ]

5 1．ウ　2．ウ　3．ア　4．ア　5．イ

6 問1．【A】ア 【B】ウ　問2．イ　問3．ウ
　問4．1．ウ　2．イ　問5．ウ　問6．end

《解 説》

1 (1)イ add five hundred to five hundred は「500＋500」という意味。
(2)ア「手を置いて, 感じる」＝「触る(touch)」　(3)イ「日曜日は土曜日
の後に来る」　(4)ア「意味や理由を知る」＝「理解する(understand)」
(5)ア Would you like to leave a message?「伝言を残されますか?」は電
話でよく使う表現。

2 1．( )の直前の文「Mary という人はいない」より, ウが適切。
2．パイを勧めた A に対し B は「結構です」と断ったからその理由を表
すアが適切。　3．( )の直後に B が Oh, you did?と答えたから( )
には過去形の文が入る。　4．( )の直前に A が食事の時間を尋ねたか
ら, レストランの開店時間を答えたイが適切。　5．( )の直後に B が
回数を答えたから, 回数を尋ねるアが適切。

3 【文章の要約】参照。(1)・call A B「AをBと呼ぶ」　(2)・lose the
use of ~「~が使えなくなる」　(3)・as much as ~ can「できる限り」
(4)( )の後の文に Wilma がバスケットボールをしたり走ったりできる
ようになった描写があるから, 彼女は歩けるようになったと考えられる。
(5)・the courage to ~「~する勇気」・work hard「熱心に取り組む」

【文章の要約】
　Wilma Rudolph は 1960 年のオリンピックの陸上競技のスター選手だっ
た。彼女は 3 つの金メダルを獲得した。人々は彼女を『世界一速い女性』
と(1)呼んだ。
　しかし, Wilma Rudolph は小さい頃, スポーツができなかった。彼女は
病弱でよく体調を崩し, そしてポリオにかかった。彼女は左脚が(2)使えな
くなり, 医師は,「彼女は二度と歩かないだろう」と言った。
　Wilma の家庭は大家族でとても貧しかったが, 彼女を助けるために(3)で
きる限りのことをした。Wilma と母親は脚の医者へ行くため, 何度も 100
キロ以上移動した。彼女の兄弟たちは毎日, 彼女の脚をマッサージした。
彼らは彼女が脚のための特別な運動をする時も手伝った。Wilma は 9 歳の
ころまでには, (4)再び歩けるようになった。すぐに彼女はバスケットボール
をしたり, 走ったりし始めた。高校で, 彼女は陸上競技のスター選手に
なり, そしてオリンピックに出場した。
　彼女は走り続け, その後 22 歳で教師兼陸上競技のコーチになった。彼
女の話は多くの人々に, 困難な状況でも(5)熱心に取り組む勇気を与えた。

4 1．… because it is one of the most beautiful countries …　・one of
＋最上級＋名詞「最も~な…のうちの1つ」　2．Yes, it's written in
the newspaper I am reading now.「それは私が今読んでいる新聞に書か
れている」という意味にする。〈be＋過去分詞〉は受け身を表す。I am
reading now が newspaper を修飾している。　3．I think listening to

music is a lot of fun.・I think＋主語＋動詞「~だと思う」・a lot of fun
「とても楽しい」　4．Could you tell me where to buy a good one?
・Could you ~?「~していただけますか?」・where to「どこで~すべ
きか」　5．…because I was too busy to watch the game …
・too … to ~「あまりに…で~できない」

5 1．5 個で 1 キロだから, 1000÷5＝200(g)　2．ジャガイモとニンジ
ンに払ったお金を求める。300＋360＝660(円)　3．肉に払った合計から
100g200 円の牛肉 200g の金額を引き, 豚肉 300g の値段を求め, 3 で割る。
(700－200×2)÷3＝100(円)　4．Mayumi は 2000 円の靴と 4000 円の
靴を『タイムセール』の時に半額で買ったから, 払った金額は(2000＋4000)
÷2＝3000(円)　5．12 時から『タイムセール』が始まる1時 30 分まで
の時間は 90 分。

【本文の要約】
　ある日, Mayumi とお母さんはデパートへ買い物に行きました。Mayumi
は靴を買いたいと思っていました。彼女は靴屋で気に入った靴を 2 足見つ
けました。1 つは 2000 円で, もう 1 つは 4000 円でした。しかし彼女は,
その店が『タイムセール』―午後 1 時 30 分から 2 時まで―を予定してい
ることを発見しました。『タイムセール』の間は, 店内のどの靴も半額にな
りました。
　ちょうど 12 時だったので, Mayumi とお母さんは食材を買うため下の
食品売り場の階へ行きました。その日, お母さんは夕食にカレーを作るつ
もりだったので, ジャガイモとニンジンと肉を買わなければなりませんで
した。八百屋ではジャガイモとニンジンが 1 キロ単位で袋に入って売られ
ていました。ジャガイモは 1 袋に 5 個入っていて, どれも 300 円で売られ
ていました。どのジャガイモもほぼ同じ大きさでした。ニンジン 4 本の袋
は 360 円でした。お母さんはジャガイモとニンジンを 1 袋ずつ買いました。
お母さんは肉も買わなければならなかったので肉屋へ行きました。その肉
屋では牛肉 100g が 200 円で売られていました。お母さんは牛肉 200g と豚
肉 300g を買い, 700 円払いました。
　食品売り場を後にし, 彼女たちは靴屋に戻りました。ちょうど『タイム
セール』が始まる時間に靴屋に入りました。Mayumi はさっき見つけた靴
を 2 足とも買いました。

6 問1．【本文の要約】参照。　問2．第2段落から数字の表記の仕方を
読み取る。1×4＋5×3＝19　問3, 4．【本文の要約】参照。
問5．第 3～4 段落でマヤ人が使っていたカレンダーを 3 つ紹介した。
問6．【本文の要約】参照。

【本文の要約】
　昔々, メキシコと中央アメリカのジャングルに住む人々の集団がいた。
彼らはマヤ人と呼ばれた。彼らの王は寺院やピラミッドを建て, [A]それら
は現在, 学者たちにとって大変重要なものとなっている。学者たちはジャ
ングルで発見された情報を使ってマヤ人の歴史や日々の暮らしを研究して
きた。彼らはマヤ文化について多くの興味深いことを発見してきた。
　マヤ人は画期的な数の数え方を知っていた。当時, 世界中のほとんどの
人が [B] 0 という数字について何も知らなかった。しかしマヤ人はその数
字を表すシンボルとして輪のような円形を使っていた。彼らの数の数え方
には 3 つのシンボルしかなかった。1 を表すのは点, 5 を表すのは棒, 0
を表すのは円形だった。マヤ人にとって重要な数字があった。たとえば
問4．1 20 という数字は手と足の指の数に等しいため特別であった。また 52
という数字もマヤ人にとって特別だった。
　マヤ人はカレンダーも作った。私たちは現在, (1)12 か月のカレンダーを
使っている。しかしマヤ人は私たちと(2)同じカレンダーを使っていなかっ

た。彼らは同時にいくつかの③違うカレンダーを使っていたのである。

問4.2Tzolkin と呼ばれるカレンダーには 13 カ月あった。どの月も 20 日あった。このカレンダーは農民が使っていた。問4.2Haab というカレンダーには 365 日あった。そのカレンダーは太陽を公転する地球の動きに基づいていた。それは 18 カ月と 5 日あった。マヤ人は最後の 5 日間は不運な日だと考えていた。マヤ人は同時にこの 2 つのカレンダーを使っていた。

またマヤ人は第 3 のカレンダーも使っていた。それは the Long Count Calendar と呼ばれた。それは紀元前 3114 年，8 月 11 日で始まっていた。彼らは世界がその日に始まったと信じていたからだ。2012 年 12 月 21 日がそのカレンダーの問6.終わりだったので，世界はその日に問6.終わると考える人もいた。

《解答》

1. 1．ninth　2．foreign　3．question　4．something
　　5．introduce

2. 1．ウ　2．イ　3．エ　4．ア　5．ア

3. 1．エ　2．ア　3．イ　4．ウ　5．イ

4. ［3番目／5番目］1．［ウ／オ］　2．［ウ／イ］　3．［カ／ア］
　　4．［イ／ウ］　5．［イ／オ］

5. 1．エ　2．ウ　3．イ　4．イ　5．ア

6. 問1．【A】ウ【B】ア【C】イ【D】ア　問2．ウ
　　問3．イ、オ　問4．hospital

《解説》

1. 1．September「9月」は1年の9番目の月。→ninth，綴りに注意。
2．Do they learn English as a foreign language at school?「日本人は学校で外国語（として）の英語を学びますか？」・as~「～として（の）」
3．That's a good question.「それはいい質問だ」　4．Would you like something to drink?「お飲み物はいかがですか？」相手の返答が予想される場合（この場合は"Yes, please."）、疑問文でも something を用いる。
5．・introduce ~self「～（自身）を紹介する」

2. 1．Aが具体的に家の様子を答えていることから判断する。　・What is ~ like?「～はどのようなものですか？」　2．・Shall I take a message?「伝言を預りましょうか？」　3．この前の授業の進度を確認する表現。Tom, where were we last time?「トム、この前はどこでしたか？」
4．・Why not?「（提案・勧誘などに同意して）そうしよう、もちろん」
5．Which part of China does she live in?「中国のどの辺りに住んでいますか？」に対する返答→ア．I think she lives in the east.「東部です」

3. 〔本文の要約〕

　1975年、田部井淳子は世界の最高峰に立っていた。彼女は絶えず山に登っている。彼女は10歳の時、級友や教師と那須山に登った。その時、自分は登山が好きだと⑴自覚した。長年にわたって、彼女は友人や家族と多くの山に登った。1971年、彼女は大きな登山計画をしていたグループに⑵加わった。彼女は毎晩ジョギングをしてその登山に備えた。1975年、彼女とそのグループはネパールに行った。一行は登山中、多くの試練に遭遇した。酸素不足から息を切らし、夜はマイナス30度の寒さに凍えた。7000mを超えるとたった300mの距離を登るのに1日かかった。⑶断念したくなる時もあったが、彼女は登り続け、⑷ついに世界最高峰、チョモランマの頂に立った。彼女はなぜ登山を愛するのか？その最適な答えは彼女の言葉に見出せる。「一歩ずつ歩けばどんな山の頂にも立つことができる。早く歩く必要はないわ。⑤ただ歩き続けるだけよ」

本文の要約を参照。⑴・find out~「～だと分かる」　⑵・join「加わる、参加する」　⑶・give up「諦める」　⑷・at last「ついに、とうとう」
⑸・only「ただ～だけ」

4. 1．I'm looking forward to going to the concert with you.　・look forward to ~ing（動名詞）「～することを楽しみに待つ」to は不定詞ではなく前置詞。従って後に続く動詞は動名詞。　2．Is this the key that you were looking for?　that は関係代名詞。・look for~「～を探す」
3．He and I have known each other since we were young.〈have/has＋過去分詞〉、現在完了の継続用法。・each other「お互い（に、を）」
4．Yes, he is a tennis player loved by many young girls in Japan.〈⑱＋過去分詞＋by~〉「～によって…された⑱」過去分詞の形容詞的用法。
5．…, but it was so expensive that I couldn't buy it.・so…that~「とても…なので～」

5. 〔本文の要約〕

　トライアスロンは、休みなく泳ぎ、自転車に乗り、走る競技である。ある日、山田氏がこのレースに参加した。男性コースは水泳が1.5 km、自転車走行が40 kmだった。レースの距離は合計51.5 kmだった。レースは朝9時に始まった。彼は水泳に30分、自転車に1時間20分かかった。そして50分走り、レースを終えた。田中氏も同じレースに参加した。彼は山田氏より5分早く水泳を終えたが、自転車では10分遅くなった。そして2人とも同時にレースを終えた。女性コースは水泳1 km、自転車とマラソンは男性コースの距離の半分である。山田夫人は女性のレースに参加した。彼女は山田氏と同じ速さで泳ぎ、自転車に乗り、走った。女性のレースは男性のレースと同じ時刻に始まった。

1．山田氏がレースを終えた時刻：9時にスタート＋水泳30分＋自転車1時間20分＋マラソン50分→11:40

2．田中氏が自転車を終えた時刻：9時にスタート＋水泳25分＋自転車1時間30分→10:55　3．田中氏のマラソン時間：11:40−10:55＝45分

4．男性コースのマラソン距離は51.5−（1.5＋40）＝10 km。女性コースのマラソン距離は男性の半分だから5 km。女性コースの総距離：水泳1 km＋自転車20 km＋マラソン5 km＝26 km

5．山田氏と山田夫人は同じ速さでレースをこなした。山田氏は水泳1.5 kmに30分、マラソン10 kmに50分かかったから、山田夫人は水泳1 kmに20分、マラソン5 kmに25分かかったことになる。水泳20分＋自転車40分＋マラソン25分＝1時間25分　9時から1時間25分後→10時25分

6. 〔本文の要約〕

Lisa：人には各々の夢の家があります。特別な場所で質素な家に住みたい人もいれば、【A】多くの生活用品を備えた大邸宅に住みたい人もいます。あなたの夢の家はどのようなものでしょうか。今晩のワールドレポートで、様々な夢の家を拝見しましょう。

John：今晩は。私は今、世界一価格の高い邸宅の前に立っています。日本出身の裕福な実業家の1人、ヤグチカズコ氏がこの家の所有者です。彼女は世界中にホテルやデパートを所有しています。この家は27階あり、十分な部屋があります。家は昨年建設されました。彼女は所有する車が多いため6階までは車専用の階です。次の階は50席ある映画室です。次の2階にはプールとジムがあります。客専用の階もあり、客は14～15階にある庭園で寛ぐことができます。建物の最上部4階は家族専用で、アラビア海のすばらしい眺めが望めます。

Lisa：すばらしい眺めですね。部屋がとても多いようですが、誰が掃除するのですか？

John：いい点に気がつきましたね。ヤグチ氏は【B】たくさんの掃除ロボットがあり，それらが全ての部屋掃除をするので，彼女は全く掃除しません。

Lisa：すばらしいわ！私も将来彼女のようなお金持ちになりたいです。ありがとう，John。次は Paul Brown のレポートです。

Paul：Paul Brown です。Carl Masterson はアメリカの自然について数多くの物語を書いた偉大なアメリカ人作家として有名です。彼は1824 年に生まれ，28 年後にはこの申し分のない家を建て住み始めました。それは彼が処女作を書いた後でした。彼は 48 歳で亡くなるまでずっとここに住んでいました。家には椅子が 3 つ，ベッド，テーブル，小さな机が 1 つずつあります。質素な家ですが，家の所在地こそ彼には重要でした。彼は森に家を建てました。家の前に美しい湖があります。この景色をご覧ください。

Lisa：美しい湖ですね。彼の家は本当に質素ですが，【C】執筆のために静かで美しい場所が必要だったと思います。次のレポートはアフリカからです。始めて下さい。David。

David：コンゴ民主共和国からのレポートです。Claude Milongo は 29 歳の有名なサッカー選手です。彼は現在フランスで活躍中ですが，2 年前ここに夢の家を建設しました。彼は 1984 年 1 月 1 日に生まれコンゴで育ちました。彼が 8 歳の時，家族でフランスに移住しました。彼は医者になりたかったのですが，有名なサッカー選手になりました。彼の夢の家はコンゴにあり，200 人収容のベッドがあります。【D】彼は自分のためではなく，故郷の人々のために夢の家を建てました。多くの医者や看護師が働いています。彼の夢の家は，問4病院(hospital)だったのです！

Lisa：彼はすばらしい夢の家を建てました！彼が世界中の人々から愛されるわけですね。さあ，皆さんの夢の家はどんなでしょうか？これで今晩のワールドレポートを終わります。お休みなさい。

問 1．要約参照。　問 2．ウ．建物は 27 階建て。この記述では 27 階以上の建物となる。　問 3．イ．Claude の家族がフランスに移住したのは，彼が生まれた 1984 年の 8 年後→1992 年　オ．Carl Masterson が生まれた1824 年の 28 年後→1852 年　問 4．要約参照。

《解　答》

1. 1. future　2. taken　3. language　4. highest
5. August　6. last

2. 1. エ　2. イ　3. ウ　4. ア　5. ウ　6. イ

3. 1. エ　2. ウ　3. エ　4. イ　5. ウ　6. ア

4. ［2番目／4番目］ 1. ［オ／ア］　2. ［イ／カ］　3. ［カ／ウ］
4. ［ア／オ］　5. ［ウ／カ］　6. ［ア／カ］

5. 問1. 1. エ　2. ア　3. ウ　問2. A. エ　B. イ　C. ウ
問3. ア. find　イ. studying　ウ. invite　エ. meeting

6. 1. ア　2. イ　3. ウ　4. ア　5. ア　6. エ

7. 問1. 【A】ア　【B】イ　【C】ウ　【D】ウ　問2. イ
問3. ウ　問4. ア. tiger　イ. break　問5. ウ　問6. イ

《解　説》

1. 1. Bが将来なりたい職業を答えている。　2. 「20年前に撮られた古い写真」で過去分詞を用いて pictures を修飾。　3. 「ほとんどの人が英語を使う」で言語。　4. 富士山の高さをつけ加えた応答。＜the＋最上級＞
5. 9月の直前の月は8月。　6. オリンピックはどのくらい続くのかの質問。

2. 1. 父親の応答で「無理しなくていいよ」からBが父親にしてあげることを申し出たと解釈。　2. Aが始発駅と終着駅をあげて説明。Bは路線(line)を尋ねたと解釈。　3. 会話の内容からBがAに贈り物を渡した場面でその会話のAの最初の発言としてウが適切。　4. Aが7時ごろと時刻を答えている。　5. Aの夕食への誘いを断る適切な理由。　6. 自転車を貸してもらえるかのAの問いかけに対するBの適切な断り方とその理由。

3. (1)planets を現在分詞を用いて修飾。　(2)受動態＜be＋過去分詞＞
(3)直前の Some animals に対して Other animals　(4)過去〜＝the last〜
(5)現在完了＜have＋過去分詞＞　(6)「を得るために」の意味 for〜

4. 並べ替えの語句のみ：1. (long does your sister practice the piano)
2. (a younger brother who lives with)
3. (don't we buy something cold to)　4. (don't want her to say that)
5. (has the power to make us)　6. (teach me how to use this)

5. 問1. (1)「とてもご親切にどうも」の意味。　(2)Jane の「カナダのバンクーバーから来た」が応答になる質問。　(3)Mari の No, I haven't で始まる応答になる質問。　問2. A. Jane の「Minato College で英語を教える」が応答になる Mari の発言。　B. Mari にあさっての夕食に誘われた Jane の発言：「今日は木曜日。明日(金曜日)は予定がある。土曜日は暇である。」　C. You're welcome はお礼に対する応答。
問3. ア. ＜help〜to＋不定詞＞に合わせ＜find a way to〜＞「〜への道をみつける」　イ. Mari の弟はバンクーバーの高校に通っている→＜be＋〜ing＞に合わせ studying　ウ. ＜decide to＋不定詞＞に合わせ＜invite〜to...＞「〜を…に招待する」　エ. 「Mari と彼女の母親に会うのを楽しみにしている」という意味で＜look forward to＋動名詞(〜ing)＞→meeting

6. 1. Takashi と Mizuki は同じ飲み物を3本ずつ購入。2人が払った金額の差600円は2人が買ったボールの数の差4個分の金額→ボールは1個150円。　2. 買ったボールの金額をそれぞれの合計金額から引くと飲み物3本分の金額。　3. 正午から4時15分までを分で計算。　4. 16個の内

3個紛失。残り13個の内8個を Takashi が、5個を Mizuki が持ち帰った。　5. 届いたボールは150個。20個はサービスで無料で送料も無料なので130個分の金額。　6. 80個×120円＋送料500円(100個以上から送料無料)

7. 問1. ［A］Cathy が述べた人々の意見に対して Dr.Jones は反論している。
［B］直前の文：「動物たちは捕えられるときケガをする」を心配する内容。
［C］直前の文：「家の中には彼らが走り回る十分な場所がない」→健康に悪い。　［D］直前の Dr. Jones の発言の最終文を Cathy が言いかえて確認している内容。　問2. in the right way「正しいやり方で」とイの follow the rules「ルールに従う」は同様の意味。　問3. ア. ○Lion の Food の内容と一致。　イ. ○African clawed frog の Other Needs の内容と一致。ウ. ×その内容の記述はない。　問4. ア. 大きい野生の猫。体に黄色と黒のしま模様。　イ. 作業の手を止めて持つ短い時間→休憩　問5. 野生動物をペットとして飼うことの安全性やその必要条件などをとりあげた討論内容からウが最も適切。　問6. ア. ×野生動物の飼育が困難な理由は「危険」だから。　イ. ○Dr. Baker の発言1文目の I don't agree と一致。　ウ. ×野生動物をかわいいと言っているのは Dr. Jones。

《英　語》

1. 1．yours　2．stopped　3．doctor　4．Saturday　5．famous
6．bought

2. 1．イ　2．ウ　3．ア　4．エ　5．ウ

3. 1．ウ　2．エ　3．ア　4．ウ　5．エ

4. 〔3番・5番目〕1．イ・オ　2．エ・オ　3．ア・カ　4．オ・エ

5. 問1．1．カ　2．ク　3．キ　4．ア　5．エ　6．イ
問2．ア．taking　イ．visit　ウ．coming　エ．worried〔worrying〕

6. 1．ウ　2．ア　3．ア　4．ウ

7. 問1．【A】エ【B】ウ　問2．エ　問3．エ（→）イ（→）ウ（→）ア
問4．ウ　問5．1．ア　2．ウ　問6．イ

【解　説】

1. 1．所有代名詞「あなたのもの」　2．雨が止んでいないのでテニスができない。　3．体の具合が悪いので診てもらう　4．月曜日の前々日
5．be famous for～「～で有名」　6．誕生日プレゼントに買ってくれた

2. 1．Bの3年間という応答を導く質問。　2．Bの全く眠らなかった，を受けてAが質問。　3．Aから来週犬の世話を頼まれたがBも同時期に不在になるので丁寧に断る応答。　4．写真撮影の許可の問いかけにBは丁寧な表現で否定の応答。　5．頻度を尋ねる質問への応答。

3. (1)be＋過去分詞＋with の受身の文　(2)否定文に続く否定での「…もまた」の意味。　(3)lucky for ～「～にとって幸運」　(4)水中で長時間する行動で stay が適切。　(5)水に含まれた酸素が出てきてできた泡。

4. 1．The trip was so wonderful that I want to visit there again. [so～that...「とても～ので...」]　2．She became the second Japanese woman to go to space.　3．But scientists have shown that this is not true. [have＋過去分詞の現在完了の文]　4．He is a baseball player who is known all over Japan. [関係代名詞 who 以下の節で baseball player を説明]

5. 問1．(1)次のSaraの応答「いいえ，ひとつも」を導く質問。　(2)次のLizの応答「日本庭園です」を導く質問。　(3)Lizの思いがけない応答に驚いたAkikoの問いかけ。　(4)Lizが日本について勉強した結果。　(5)LizとSaraが日本での抱負を語った。2人へのAkikoの発言を考える。　(6)Saraの指摘に同意する応答。　問2．(ア)take by car「車で連れていく」・is＋動詞の ing で現在進行形。　(イ)3番目のSaraの発言 want to go to～と同じ意味の語。　(ウ)Lizは来日前に日本のことを学んだ。before＋動名詞（～ing）　(エ)Saraは車があまり進んでいないので心配[be worried]

6. 1．家を出発して30分（$\frac{1}{2}$時間）後に父は西に60kmの半分，兄は東に80kmの半分まで進んだ⇒30＋40＝70km。　2．80km/hの兄の車で出かけ9時45分（$\frac{3}{4}$時間後）に車を降りその後西に2km歩いた。80×$\frac{3}{4}$－2＝58km。　3．父と兄は同じ距離を走った。兄が11時に目的地に到着⇒全走行距離160km。60km/hの父の車は11時の時点で120km走行⇒残り40km。それを時間に直す。　4．父の車では家まで（160km）戻るのに2$\frac{2}{3}$時間かかるが兄の車では2時間。2人が同時に帰宅したということは兄は2$\frac{2}{3}$時間の休憩をとったことになる。

7. 問1．[A]後に「太陽熱を利用した調理の始まり」の文。[B]後に続く内容から太陽の光が室内を暖めることを意味する。　問2．大きさが異なる5つの正方形の箱を順に内側に入れた図。　問3．1．箱を置く。2．そこに置いた理由。3．各箱の中の温度を測る。4．温度測定の結果。問4．設問の文が「しかし今では」と始まるのでそれと比較する以前の様子を述べた文に続けるのが最も自然。　問5．1．第2段落最終行に答。2．最終段落で調理用に木を集める必要がなくなり生活が楽になったとある。　問6．ア．ガラスの箱での solar cooking は約250年前の実験から－×。　イ．De Saussure の実験内容と一致。　ウ．実験の結果，全ての箱に太陽光が通っている－×。　エ．solar cooking に木は不要。

《英　語》

1. 1．different　2．present　3．vacation　4．front　5．wrong
6．skiing〔snowboarding〕

2. 1．ウ　2．ア　3．イ　4．エ　5．ウ

3. 1．エ　2．イ　3．エ　4．ア　5．ウ

4. 〔3番・5番目〕1．ウ・イ　2．ア・エ　3．カ・イ　4．イ・オ

5. 問1．1．エ　2．オ　3．キ　4．ウ　5．ア　6．ク　　問2．1．broken
2．excited　3．found　4．forgot〔forgotten〕

6. 〔A〕1．ウ　2．エ　　〔B〕1．ア　2．ア　3．ウ

7. 問1．ウ　問2．【A】エ【B】ア　問3．1．ウ　2．ア
3．エ　4．イ

【解　説】

1. 1．・be different from～＝「～と違った」　2．「クリスマスのプレゼント」＝Christmas present　3．「夏休み」＝summer vacation　4．・in front of＝「～の正面に」　5．・I'm afraid you have the wrong number.＝「（電話で）番号をお間違えのようですが…」　6．雪山で遊ぶもの→スキー，スノーボードなどを答える。・Why don't we～?＝「～しませんか」・go skiing（snowboarding）＝「スキー（スノーボード）に行く」goの後は動名詞が続く。

2. 省略

3. 1．・stop ~ing「～することをやめる」　2．当時のポーランドでは女性は大学に入学できなかったので，別の国（＝another country）に行く必要があった。　3・4．Manya は Bronya に，最初に（＝first）パリへ行くよう勧め，自分は働いてその学費を送る（＝send）と言った。　5・6年後（＝six years later）

4. (1)How much will you give me for this shirt?　(2)I thought it was fifty dollars or more.　(3)He took twenty dollars out of his pocket.　(4)But I believed that was too much money.

5. 問1．1．「（CDプレイヤーが）作動しません」・work＝「（機械が）作動する」　2．「レシートは持っていません」　3．「バッグに（レシートが）ありました」　4．「（当然）それは作動するものと思っていました」　5．「しかし，試してみるのがいいと思いますよ」　6．「後ろにあるこの小さいスイッチがわかりますね?」　問2．1．・be broken＝「壊れている」　2．・get excited＝「興奮する」　3．・find out＝「～と分かる」　4．・forget to～＝「～するのを忘れる」

6. 〔A〕1．「犬のタローは家に戻るにどの位（の距離を）移動しましたか?」→第2段落参照。オーストラリアの犬のトムは1,600km，アメリカの猫のサムはトムより800km以上（＝2,400km）を移動した。日本の犬のタローはサムの半分（＝1,200km）を移動したと述べられている。　2．「伝書バトは方向を知るために何を使いますか?」→最後の行参照。「地球の磁力（の方向）」を使う
〔B〕1．「2010年3月31日以前のNassau Collegeでの20時間のレッスンはいくらですか?」→左側の広告参照。1レッスンは2時間で$40である。20時間のレッスンは，（20÷2）×40＝400で$400，これに3月末まで半額のテキスト代$20（$40÷2）を足すので合計$420。　2．「3月末まで水曜日の10時間英語レッスンはいくらですか?」→広告の右側参照。1レッスンは1時間で$25，3月末まで2時間の無料レッスンがあるので，25×（10－2）＝200で$200。　3．Nassau College, Hutchinson ともに土曜日の英語レッスンを行う。

7. 問1．These spiders cannot hurt you any more than a bee can（hurt you）.「これらのクモは蜂（があなたを傷つける）以上にあなたを傷つけることはできない」→ウ　問2．【A】直後に「虫に飛びつき捕食するクモ」の例があることから，エ「しかし，虫を捕まえるためにクモの巣を張らないクモもいる」が適切。　【B】話の前後から判断。ア「この（ブラックウィドウという）クモはしょっちゅう人を傷つける訳ではない」が適切。　問3．1．第4段落2行目参照。クモは人間にとって益虫。　2．第5段落1～2行目参照。　3．第7段落参照。　4．第2段落3～4行目参照。

解答用紙

解答用紙はキリトリ線に沿って、切り取ってお使い下さい。

平成31年度入学者選抜学力検査解答用紙　英語

氏名を記入しなさい。

氏名

受検番号を記入し、受検番号と一致した
マーク部分を塗りつぶしなさい。

受 検 番 号				
万位	千位	百位	十位	一位

解 答 欄

1
(1)
(2)
(3)
(4)
(5)

2
1
2
3
4
5

3
問1 (1) (2) (3) (4) (5) (6)
問2

4
1　3番目 5番目
2　3番目 5番目
3　3番目 5番目
4　3番目 5番目
5　3番目 5番目

5
1
2
3
4
5

6
問1
問2
問3
問4
問5
問6
問7

1 2点×5
2 3点×5
3 3点×8
4 3点×5
5 3点×5
6 3点×7

注意事項

1 解答には、必ずHBの黒鉛筆を使用し、「マーク部分
　塗りつぶしの見本」のとおりに○を塗りつぶすこと。

2 解答を訂正するときは、きれいに消して、消しくずを
　残さないこと。

3 指定された欄以外を塗りつぶしたり、文字を記入し
　たりしないこと。

4 汚したり、折り曲げたりしないこと。

良い例	マーク部分塗りつぶしの見本	
●	悪い例	
	レ点　棒　薄い　はみ出し　丸囲み	

平成30年度入学者選抜学力検査解答用紙　英語

氏名を記入しなさい。

氏名	

受検番号を記入し、受検番号と一致した
マーク部分を塗りつぶしなさい。

受　検　番　号

万位	千位	百位	十位	一位
⓪	⓪	⓪	⓪	⓪
①	①	①	①	①
②	②	②	②	②
③	③	③	③	③
④	④	④	④	④
⑤	⑤	⑤	⑤	⑤
⑥	⑥	⑥	⑥	⑥
⑦	⑦	⑦	⑦	⑦
⑧	⑧	⑧	⑧	⑧
⑨	⑨	⑨	⑨	⑨

注意事項

1 解答には、必ずHBの黒鉛筆を使用し、「マーク部分
塗りつぶしの見本」のとおりに◯を塗りつぶすこと。

2 解答を訂正するときは、きれいに消して、消しくずを
残さないこと。

3 指定された欄以外を塗りつぶしたり、文字を記入し
たりしないこと。

4 汚したり、折り曲げたりしないこと。

マーク部分塗りつぶしの見本

良い例	悪い例			
●	◑	◖	◔	○
	レ点	棒	薄い	丸囲み
			はみ出し	

解答欄

1

(1)	㋐ ㋑ ㋒ ㋓
(2)	㋐ ㋑ ㋒ ㋓
(3)	㋐ ㋑ ㋒ ㋓
(4)	㋐ ㋑ ㋒ ㋓
(5)	㋐ ㋑ ㋒ ㋓
(6)	㋐ ㋑ ㋒ ㋓
(7)	㋐ ㋑ ㋒ ㋓
(8)	㋐ ㋑ ㋒ ㋓
(9)	㋐ ㋑ ㋒ ㋓
(10)	㋐ ㋑ ㋒ ㋓

2

1	㋐ ㋑ ㋒ ㋓
2	㋐ ㋑ ㋒ ㋓
3	㋐ ㋑ ㋒ ㋓
4	㋐ ㋑ ㋒ ㋓
5	㋐ ㋑ ㋒ ㋓

3

問1	(1)	㋐ ㋑ ㋒ ㋓
	(2)	㋐ ㋑ ㋒ ㋓
	(3)	㋐ ㋑ ㋒ ㋓
	(4)	㋐ ㋑ ㋒ ㋓
	(5)	㋐ ㋑ ㋒ ㋓
	(6)	㋐ ㋑ ㋒ ㋓
問2	1	㋐ ㋑ ㋒ ㋓ ㋔ ㋕
	2	㋐ ㋑ ㋒ ㋓ ㋔ ㋕

4

1	3番目	㋐ ㋑ ㋒ ㋓ ㋔ ㋕
	5番目	㋐ ㋑ ㋒ ㋓ ㋔ ㋕
2	3番目	㋐ ㋑ ㋒ ㋓ ㋔ ㋕
	5番目	㋐ ㋑ ㋒ ㋓ ㋔ ㋕
3	3番目	㋐ ㋑ ㋒ ㋓ ㋔ ㋕
	5番目	㋐ ㋑ ㋒ ㋓ ㋔ ㋕
4	3番目	㋐ ㋑ ㋒ ㋓ ㋔ ㋕
	5番目	㋐ ㋑ ㋒ ㋓ ㋔ ㋕
5	3番目	㋐ ㋑ ㋒ ㋓ ㋔ ㋕
	5番目	㋐ ㋑ ㋒ ㋓ ㋔ ㋕

5

1	㋐ ㋑ ㋒ ㋓
2	㋐ ㋑ ㋒ ㋓
3	㋐ ㋑ ㋒ ㋓
4	㋐ ㋑ ㋒ ㋓
5	㋐ ㋑ ㋒ ㋓

6

問1	㋐ ㋑ ㋒ ㋓
問2	㋐ ㋑ ㋒ ㋓
問3	㋐ ㋑ ㋒ ㋓
問4	㋐ ㋑ ㋒ ㋓
問5	㋐ ㋑ ㋒ ㋓
問6	㋐ ㋑ ㋒ ㋓
問7	㋐ ㋑ ㋒ ㋓

1	1点×10
2	3点×5
3	問1…3点×6 問2…3点×2
4	3点×5
5	3点×5
6	3点×7

キリトリ線

平成29年度入学者選抜学力検査解答用紙　英語

キリトリ線

氏名を記入しなさい。

氏名	

受検番号を記入し、受検番号と一致した
マーク部分を塗りつぶしなさい。

受 検 番 号 欄

万位	千位	百位	十位	一位
⓪	⓪	⓪	⓪	⓪
①	①	①	①	①
②	②	②	②	②
③	③	③	③	③
④	④	④	④	④
⑤	⑤	⑤	⑤	⑤
⑥	⑥	⑥	⑥	⑥
⑦	⑦	⑦	⑦	⑦
⑧	⑧	⑧	⑧	⑧
⑨	⑨	⑨	⑨	⑨

解 答 欄

（解答欄はマークシート形式：各設問 ⑦ ⑦ ⑦ ⑦ などのマーク欄）

1：(1)～(10)

2：1～5

3：問1 (1)～(6)、問2 1～2

4：1～5（各3番目・5番目）

5：1～5

6：問1～問7

注意事項

1　解答には、必ずHBの黒鉛筆を使用し、「マーク部分塗りつぶしの見本」を参考に〇を塗りつぶすこと。
2　解答を訂正するときは、きれいに消して、消しくずを残さないこと。
3　指定された欄以外を塗りつぶしたり、文字を記入したりしないこと。
4　汚したり、折り曲げたりしないこと。

マーク部分塗りつぶしの見本		
良い例	悪い例	
●	い点 薄い	棒 はみ出し 〇丸囲み

配点

設問	配点
1	1点×10
2	3点×5
3	問1…3点×6 問2…3点×2
4	3点×5
5	3点×5
6	3点×7

平成28年度入学者選抜学力検査解答用紙　英語

氏名 _____

※100点満点

配点
- 1 　2点×8
- 4 　各 完答3点×5
- 他 　3点×23

マーク上の注意事項
1　HBの黒鉛筆を使って，○の中を正確に塗りつぶすこと。
　　それ以外の筆記用具でのマークは，解答が無効になる場合があります。
2　答えを直すときは，きれいに消して，消しくずを残さないこと。
3　決められた欄以外にマークしたり，記入したりしないこと。
4　汚したり折り曲げたりしてはいけません。

良い例	悪い例				
●	✓レ点	棒	薄い	はみ出し	丸囲み

1

	⑦	④	⑦	⑨
(1)	⑦	④	⑦	⑨
(2)	⑦	④	⑦	⑨
(3)	⑦	④	⑦	⑨
(4)	⑦	④	⑦	⑨
(5)	⑦	④	⑦	⑨
(6)	⑦	④	⑦	⑨
(7)	⑦	④	⑦	⑨
(8)	⑦	④	⑦	⑨

4

			⑦	④	⑦	⑨	⑦	⑰
1	3番目		⑦	④	⑦	⑨	⑦	⑰
	5番目		⑦	④	⑦	⑨	⑦	⑰
2	3番目		⑦	④	⑦	⑨	⑦	⑰
	5番目		⑦	④	⑦	⑨	⑦	⑰
3	3番目		⑦	④	⑦	⑨	⑦	⑰
	5番目		⑦	④	⑦	⑨	⑦	⑰
4	3番目		⑦	④	⑦	⑨	⑦	⑰
	5番目		⑦	④	⑦	⑨	⑦	⑰
5	3番目		⑦	④	⑦	⑨	⑦	⑰
	5番目		⑦	④	⑦	⑨	⑦	⑰

2

	⑦	④	⑦	⑨
1	⑦	④	⑦	⑨
2	⑦	④	⑦	⑨
3	⑦	④	⑦	⑨
4	⑦	④	⑦	⑨
5	⑦	④	⑦	⑨

5

	⑦	④	⑦	⑨
1	⑦	④	⑦	⑨
2	⑦	④	⑦	⑨
3	⑦	④	⑦	⑨
4	⑦	④	⑦	⑨
5	⑦	④	⑦	⑨

3

	⑦	④	⑦	⑨
(1)	⑦	④	⑦	⑨
(2)	⑦	④	⑦	⑨
(3)	⑦	④	⑦	⑨
(4)	⑦	④	⑦	⑨
(5)	⑦	④	⑦	⑨
(6)	⑦	④	⑦	⑨

6

	⑦	④	⑦
問1	⑦	④	⑦
問2	⑦	④	⑦
問3	⑦	④	⑦
問4	⑦	④	⑦
問5	⑦	④	⑦
問6	⑦	④	⑦
問7	⑦	④	⑦

キリトリ線

	受 検
受検地	番 号
氏 名	

英 語

6 問 6. 4 点
他. 各 3 点

総 得 点	
	※100点満点

得 点

1
(1) **e** | | | | |
(2) **m** | | | | |
(3) **g** | | | |
(4) **f** | | | |
(5) **i** | | | | | | |

1 | |

2
1 | 2 | 3 | 4 | 5

2 | |

3
(1) | (2) | (3) | (4) | (5)

3 | |

4

	3番目	5番目
1		

	3番目	5番目
2		

	3番目	5番目
3		

	3番目	5番目
4		

	3番目	5番目
5		

各完答

4 | |

5
1 | 2 | 3 | 4 | 5

5 | |

6
問 1 【A】 | 【B】

問 2 | 問 3

問 4 1 | 2 問 5

問 6 **n** | | | |

6 | |

キ リ ト リ 線

受検地		受 検 番 号	
氏　名			

平成 26 年度入学者選抜学力検査解答用紙

英　語

総　得　点	
	※100点満点

得　点		
1		

1
(1) t
(2) t
(3) S
(4) u
(5) m

2

1		2		3		4		5	

得点		
2		

3

(1)		(2)		(3)		(4)		(5)	

3		

4

	3番目	5番目
1		

	3番目	5番目
2		

	3番目	5番目
3		

	3番目	5番目
4		

	3番目	5番目
5		

4		

5

1		2		3		4		5	

5		

6

問 1

【A】		【B】	

問 2 　　　　　　問 3

問 4

1		2	

問 5

問 6

6		

6 　問 6．4 点　　他．各 3 点

平成 25 年度入学者選抜学力検査解答用紙

英　　語

総　　得　　点	
	※100点満点

得　点

1

1		2		3	

4		5	

1

2

1		2		3		4		5	

2

3

1		2		3		4		5	

3

4

	3番目	5番目		3番目	5番目		3番目	5番目
1			2			3		

	3番目	5番目		3番目	5番目
4			5		

4

5

1		2		3		4		5	

5

6　問 1

【A】		【B】		【C】		【D】	

6

問 2

問 3

問 4

6 問4　4点　他 各3点

キ
リ
ト
リ
線

平成 24 年度入学者選抜学力検査解答用紙

英　語

総　得　点	
	※100点満点

得　点

1

1		2		3	
4		5		6	

1 | | |

2

1		2		3		4		5		6	

2 | | |

3

1		2		3		4		5		6	

3 | | |

4

	1	2	3	4	5	6
2番目						
4番目						

4 | | |

※各完答

5

問 1

1		2		3	

問 2

A		B		C	

問 3

ア		イ	
ウ		エ	

5 | | |

6

1		2		3		4		5		6	

6 | | |

7

問 1

【A】		【B】		【C】		【D】	

問 2 | | 　　問 3 | |

問 4

ア		イ	

問 5 | | 　　問 6 | |

7 | | |

各 2 点

平成 23 年度入学者選抜学力検査解答用紙

英　　語

総　得　点	
	※100点満点

得　点

1

1		2		3	
4		5		6	

各2点　**1**

2

1		2		3		4		5	

各2点　**2**

3

1		2		3		4		5	

各2点　**3**

4

	1	2	3	4
完答（ 3番目				
5番目				

各3点　**4**

5　問1

1		2		3		4		5		6	

各2点　**5**

問2

ア		イ	
ウ		エ	

6

1		2		3		4	

各3点　**6**

7　問1

【A】	【B】

問2 □

各3点　**7**

問3

1	→	2	→	3	→	4
	→		→		→	完答

問4 □　　問5 | 1 | | 2 | |　　問6 □

117

平成 22 年度入学者選抜学力検査解答用紙

総　　得　　点	
	※100点満点

英　　語

1 各2点

1		2		3	
4		5		6	

1	
得点	

2 各2点

1		2		3		4		5	

2	
得点	

3 各2点

1		2		3		4		5	

3	
得点	

4 各3点

	1	2	3	4
完答（ 3番目 5番目				

4	
得点	

5 各2点

問 1

1		2		3		4		5		6	

問 2

1		2		3	
4					

5	
得点	

6 各3点

〔A〕

1		2	

〔B〕

1		2		3	

6	
得点	

7 各3点

問 1

問 2

【A】		【B】	

問 3

1		2		3		4	

7	
得点	

― MEMO ―

— MEMO —